Rev. Edward J.
635 7 Beech Daly Rd.
TAYLOR, MICH. 48180

I COR. 13   J. Sidlow BAXTER

Vs. 1-3 The utter necessity of love
Vs. 4-7 The moral excellency of love
Vs. 8-13 The abiding supremacy of love

AND THE GREATEST OF THESE

AND
THE
GREATEST
OF
THESE

THE POWER OF CHRISTIAN
LOVE

George Sweeting

FLEMING H. REVELL COMPANY
OLD TAPPAN · NEW JERSEY

Dedicated to my loving wife
HILDA MARGRET SWEETING
whose life and patience
have been an inspiration to me

Introduction

Who could say that this word about the love the
Bible speaks about is not needed? We need such a word
again and again. Faith is indeed the basic virtue, but love
is the crowning one. We thank our brother for a plain,
practical and pointed word on this important subject.
Most of all we appreciate his emphasis on the divine
origin of love.

We say with Bishop Wordsworth:

> Gracious Spirit, Holy Ghost,
> Taught by Thee we covet most,
> Of Thy gifts at Pentecost,
> Holy, heavenly love.
> Love is kind, and suffers long;
> Love is meek and thinks no wrong;
> Love than death itself more strong;
> Therefore give us love.

William Culbertson
President, Moody Bible Institute

Contents

love and doctrine WALK TOGETHER

Preface

God's love is powerful beyond human understanding. This very generation could be won by demonstrating this love in deed and word. The redemptive word of God must also show itself in a redemptive work to needy people.

William Shakespeare wrote:

But love is blind, and lovers cannot see
The pretty faults that themselves commit.

The love we speak of in this book is discerning, for love and doctrine walk together. There can be no disjunction between these two.

"My prayer for you is that you will overflow more and more with love for others, and at the same time keep on growing in spiritual knowledge and insight, For I want you always to see clearly the difference between right and wrong, and to be inwardly clean, no one being able to criticize you from now until our Lord returns" (Philippians 1:9, 10).

This book is written so that many may follow "a more excellent way."

George Sweeting

I. THE SEARCH FOR LOVE

I

The Search for Love

As I sit here writing at my desk in Chicago's historic Moody Church, this city of four million people is paralyzed under two feet of snow. Beyond my frosted windows the broad boulevards and expressways, usually teeming with traffic, are deserted—transformed by the windblown drifts into long, unbroken sweeps of white. Here and there, as snow fell steadily during the day, I could see a modern pioneer venturing beyond his own front door. In the warm security of my office, I found myself speculating as to what had motivated him to slowly, tediously shovel his way outdoors: the spirit of adventure? the instinct of self-preservation? or concern for others?

Night is falling now, and the most vigorous people have already struggled free of the storm's grip. "Hello, there! How are you doing?" rings across the street between neighbors who heretofore have scarcely spoken. A blizzard has a unique ability to transform a big, impersonal city into small-town friendliness. My favorite radio newscaster, reporting on the storm, commented on this and added that this sort of mass emergency always brings out both the best and the worst in human beings. The day's news items confirmed this. In one end of the city an impromptu chain of command grew into a neighborhood crew of one hundred fifty people, shoveling in teams of three, to release their families from the blizzard's clutch. An energetic gang of high-school boys worked under police supervision digging out seventy-five buried automobiles and hauling several ill persons by toboggan to waiting ambulances. Twenty-five girls in the same suburb did volunteer duty in two hospitals to replace regular staff members who were snowbound in their homes.

At the same time, elsewhere in Chicago, a truck driver was held captive in the cab of his own stalled truck while a crowd carried off twenty thousand pounds of meat. A group of youths and housewives looted a stalled soft-drink truck of two hundred cases of beverages, which they dragged by sled to their housing project.

This constant struggle between selfishness and kindness has crippled man's potential since human history began, for man has an astounding capacity for both selfishness and love. When forced into a situation that threatens him, he will frighten even himself by his ability to cheat and steal and lie. But his most satisfying moments come, quite unexpectedly, when he finds himself spontaneously doing something for someone else.

We can all remember the warm experience of such moments: the annual glow that settles briefly over the world at Christmastime; the surge of caring that buoys up the bereaved when death has struck; the thoughtfulness of a housewife who does an invalid neighbor's marketing along with her own. We are touched when we see our elder child help a younger sister with her homework, or see our youngest reach out in unexpected

14

sympathy to comfort a hurt playmate. We feel a little better about the younger generation when we watch the boys next door put up the storm windows for the widow across the way; a little better about adults when our neighborhood chips in to buy a wheelchair for someone in need, or the family down the road opens its arms to an unhappy foster child. All of us have experienced the surge of well-being that fills our inner selves when we burst free of our own self-concern to bring pleasure to another.

And all of us know, too, the occasional moments of shamed awareness that we do this too seldom. "I don't understand myself at all," wrote Paul, "for I really want to do what is right, but I can't. I do what I don't want to. . . . It seems to be a fact of life that when I want to do what is right, I inevitably do what is wrong" (Romans 7:15, 21). Perhaps no single factor has so limited the church down through the years as man's inhumanity to man—sometimes deliberate cruelty, but far more often sheer indifference.

This matter of relationships between people has become of such concern to psychologists and others that our century is sometimes called the Age of Human Relations. Our relationships with others are incredibly unmanageable, and we can never consistently improve them until we have first rearranged our own inner direction—away from self, and toward God. There is a very good reason for the order in which Christ stated His two great commandments—the second is just impossible without the first! Love of neighbor can only become a real experience for us as we love the Lord our God with all our hearts, souls and minds.

15

I have sometimes thought that life can be compared to a production line. From birth to death man produces good and bad, love and hate, beauty and ugliness, energy and boredom, order and chaos—often in rather direct proportion to how he is getting along with his wife! Our feeling of worth is directly related to our meaningful personal relationships.

You may have been shaken, as I was, by a small newspaper item recently about a fourteen-year-old boy who took his own life because "no one seemed to care." He had felt no relationship, no sense of love from any creature but his dog, and in a brief suicide note addressed to his parents he left instructions for its care.

No one seemed to care. What a stark summation of our world's lack of love—or lack of communication. Quite likely that boy's parents did love him, but they evidently never let him know it, and his death illustrated sharply how minor deeds of lovelessness (*undeeds* might be a better description) add up to major tragedies. This is no revolutionary statement of fresh truth; it is a heartbreak we have with us always. Frustration, loneliness, self-pity, indifference, emptiness, hostility, hatred, closeheartedness, resentment, jealousy, and the resultant criminal acts and the ills of mind and body, all grow like rank weeds to fill the holes gouged in the human spirit when nobody seems to care.

People of all ages and cultures have a sensitivity to genuine love and concern, and when these come through with unmistakable clarity, an amazing, mysterious energy leaps forth in response. And God, who is love, once again is revealed through the act of human loving.

"When you refused to help the least of these My

16

brothers," Jesus said, "you were refusing to help Me" (Matthew 25:45). He told His followers, "If you love only those who love you, what good is that? . . . If you are friendly only with your friends, how are you different from anybody else?" (Matthew 5:46, 47). But the nagging question remains: How to do it?

The good news of the gospel lies not in words or creeds, but in power. One of the reasons for Christ's not remaining on earth in human form seems to have been that more power would be available to all men through the gift of the Holy Spirit. ". . . when the Father sends the Comforter to represent Me—and by the Comforter I mean the Holy Spirit—He will teach you much more as well as remind you of everything I Myself have told you" (John 14:26). ". . . when the Holy Spirit has come upon you, you will receive power . . ." (Acts 1:8).

To the Christian, whose whole life has come aglow with the sense of God's love, there is nothing more important than learning how to love others. Do you remember the story of Jesus and the rich young man? The youth had obeyed all the commandments of his Jewish tradition, but when Jesus told him to give his money to the poor—a supreme test of love in his case—he turned away sadly. The disciples who had overheard the conversation were aghast. "Who in the world can be saved?" they asked. And Jesus looked at them intently. "Humanly speaking, no one! But with God, everything is possible" (Matthew 19:25, 26). The Bible is very clear on the point that if we have money enough to live well, and don't share it with others in need, it is questionable whether God's love is in us at all.

"Little children, let us stop just *saying* we love people;

17

let us *really* love them, and *show it* by our *actions*"
(I John 3:18).

Come with me through the pages that follow. Examine
with me the nature of God's love, and our human reflection of it to others. Learn with me how to lay hold on
the power of God that does make loving possible.

I JOHN 3:18

II. FOLLOW AFTER LOVE

II

Follow After Love

Love is work. Even the most winsome person becomes exasperating sooner or later. Just about the time you decide you have finally loved someone enough, you discover in a flare of hostility that you still have a long way to go.

Whether it is your toddler who has just spilled ink all over your best chair, or your mother-in-law who is stubborn about taking a complete phone message when you are out, you learn that your natural love wears out. It simply is not enough.

When your two-year-old is nodding in his high chair, your warm feeling of love for him nearly melts your buttons. But when he's out of the high chair and into a wastebasket, you know something has to come to your aid, if your feelings are going to stay sweet!

Perhaps you are without relations, and your life just moves matter-of-factly from one day to the next. You are not aware of tests of your ability to love, because you are not close to anyone. Then one day something happens—you realize you are out of touch, alone. You have no one to love, no one who cares much about you. You do not know how to love. Maybe you are not even sure what love is. Perhaps a college romance once shat-

21

tered your dreams, and you decided then that you would not get hurt again.

The word *love* is too commonly tossed about. You may just *love* pancakes; your daughter may *love* to ski; the girl next door may be head over heels in *love* with your son; you may sing solemnly in church about "Love divine, all loves excelling"; your community may express its *love* to a fire victim by meeting hospital expenses.

The English language seems poor, indeed, when it comes to talking about preference (love), romance (love), affection (love), compassion (love), enjoyment (love), and relationship to Almighty God (love). Throughout this book we will be using the word *love* to mean the cohesive force that holds man to his God and to his fellow human beings.

"Love is exclusively a Person," says Norman Grubb in his book, *The Key to Everything*. "God is love." And the only reason for our human existence is to contain Him. How many times the Bible calls us vessels. A vessel is a hollow object made to hold something; God has made human beings to be His vessels, and He expects us to contain Him. How very useless a hollow object is when it remains empty!

If our whole function in life is to contain Him, to be filled with love, then we are wise to get on with the supreme business for which we were created. Making love the prime object of living is appropriate for every individual, whether a grandmother, a tool and die maker, a coed, or a defense attorney.

None of us had anything to do with being born into this world, yet we are alive. We all possess this thing called life. Our time on earth is extremely short. Life is pictured as a falling leaf, a fading flower, a darting shadow, a flying arrow, a pursuing eagle, a moving shuttle, or a vanishing vapor—here and gone. Our earthly life is so short that the cradle wood feels the marble of the tomb.

It is impossible to read all the books, see all the sights, hear all the people and include all the possibilities of life. Our real problem is one of selection. We constantly *Selection* strive to choose the very best, to go after the greatest good. It is not enough for us to work hard; only as we work in the right direction do we find satisfaction. We need to learn how to recognize and avoid the detours if we are to make progress on the main road.

The Apostle Paul, in writing to the church at Corinth, listed many good ways of living, but he concludes that the way of love is "a more excellent way" (I Corinthians 12:31, KJV). He plainly announces that love is better and greater than any other possible gift. The scholar Beets renders this Bible phrase, "a surpassingly good way I show you." Lias translates it, "I show you an eminently excellent way."

Peter came to the same conclusion: he taught the early church many things, but he too rated love as the very best way of life. "Above all hold unfailing your love for one another, since love covers a multitude of sins" (I Peter 4:8, RSV). Peter encouraged them, "above all," to give themselves to love.

It was during the first century after Christ that Tertullian, one of the early Christian theologians wrote: "It is our care for the helpless, our practice of loving kindness, that brands us in the eyes of many of our opponents.

23

'Look!' they say. 'How they love one another! Look how they are prepared to die for one another.'"

Many of the early Christians followed the practice of setting aside a room in the home to be reserved for people in need. They called these Christ Rooms. This extension of God's love to other people in the form of hospitality was accepted in that day as a serious responsibility. Those early Christians teach us, surrounded by today's modern paganism, an important lesson: it was their style of living that convinced their neighbors in those Greek and Roman cities about the divinity of this Jesus they followed. Some super-power was *in* them. They were vessels containing unusual love.

Tradition tells us about the aged Apostle John, bidding farewell to his congregation. He encouraged them, as he had often done, to love one another. The people then, like people today, had heard these words so often that they nodded carelessly. Everything was wrapped up in that one bundle of love—to God and to man. John challenged his people to keep on the main road of love. All three New Testament writers—Peter, Paul, and John —describe love as the greatest goal of life.

I once heard of an artist who was commissioned to design a trademark. After some time he submitted his design and a bill for $500. The design was unusually simple, and the client questioned the artist on the steep price. "The charge is for knowing what to leave out," answered the artist. In the business of everyday living, it is very important to know what to leave out. There are so many things to absorb us, to use up our time and our energies. We must learn to leave out the trivialities and concentrate on the essentials.

24

Emerson wrote, "Give all to love. . . ." Love is the lubricating oil for the problems of life. Love can win over lawlessness. Love is the only cure for hate. Love is color blind to skin. Love is God's healing balm for the individual soul as well as for the world. Love is God's answer to man's problem. Love is the supreme good.

The Greek language has words for three different dimensions of love. The first is *eros*, or self-gratifying love. This is a physical expression of love. It is pleasurable, but often self-centered, and relatively short-lived. We could call it sex love, and the misuse of it is lust. C. S. Lewis says eros is "that kind of love which lovers are in." Eros—ask any schoolgirl—is strong, sweet and terrifying! It needs help, or it dies or becomes a demon.

The second is *philia*, or companionate love. This is the love which exists between good friends, or between parents and children. Let us call it affection. We feel this only for people with whom we are familiar. We don't always know when affection begins; often we discover only after someone has gone how fond we were of him. By itself, philia is a quiet, comfortable feeling for people we usually take for granted. Probably much of the solid happiness we experience in our natural lives comes from our humble affections for each other. But philia too needs a far higher sort of love than it can ever be by itself.

This third sort of love is *agape*, unselfish, sacrificial love. This is the word which speaks of God's love for us and in us. This word is seldom found in classical Greek, as the pagan world was unaware of its power or reality. The foundation of this love is God Himself, and we see this love demonstrated at Bethlehem's manger and Calvary's cross. This is the love we need desperately in order to make sense out of the others; this is the love that brings real stature and glory to eros and philia. Without God's help, our other loves cannot even remain what they start out to be, or become what they promise. For the first time, as God's love pours into us, other loves in our lives receive a firm foundation.

One woman I know tells how all her life she had been hungry for love. As a child she would do anything to win approval from her friends and her family. She wanted her mother to hug her, her father to buy her expensive tokens of his love. Immediately after high-school graduation she married, but her relationship with her husband never got beyond the physical level, and she knew she still had not found any satisfying love. They had one baby after another, and she began to live for her four children. The torment was tearing her up inside, and nothing seemed to help. Then a mere acquaintance invited her to a Bible class in her home, and she heard the good news that Christ loved her. Suddenly she sensed that here was the love she had been looking for all her life—here was someone who loved her just as she was, and whose only design was her own good. She began at last to come alive.

But this woman was still overwhelmed with aware-ness of the gulf between her husband and God. Then one day she heard her friend say, "Now that you know Christ you will want to represent Him in your home. God changes us as He works in the lives of those we love." Gradually she realized how many things needed changing in her life. There was her loud, nagging voice

—the Spirit of God in her taught her how to hold her tongue. Her housekeeping improved. Her meals showed more interest and originality. She worked off excess pounds. Instead of going back to bed after her husband left for work, she stayed up and enjoyed a good breakfast with the children, and had prayer and Bible reading with them before the school bus came.

As God's love kept softening and changing her, the woman's love for her husband and children expressed itself in ways that softened and affected them. One day her husband went out the door, and then turned around and came back. He took her in his arms and kissed her good-bye, something he had not done for years.

And what a delight as she tucked her five-year-old into bed to hear her say, "Mommy, it's so nice since we came to love Jesus, isn't it?"

Only in His name can our human loves blossom with beauty and security.

Heavenly Father, we openly admit our need of love. We see this gift as the most excellent way. Thy love is like heavenly oil to overcome the frictions of earth. Thy love is the cure for hate and the remedy for lawlessness. Thy love is color blind. Thy love has saved us and sustains us each passing day. We thank Thee for such grace.

This day we would vow a vow to follow after love. We recognize this grace as supreme. May we guard against all that would hinder us in this daily pursuit. Let us permit nothing to deflect us from this surpassingly good way. We see Thy love as the pinnacle, the apogee, of all grace. Help us, dear Lord, to follow daily after love. All this we pray in the loving name of Jesus Christ our Saviour. Amen.

III. LOVE IS THE FOUNDATION

III

Love Is the Foundation

Love is the foundation of all that is worthwhile in life. Love for each member of the family is the basis of the home, and a reflection of the greater fellowship with the Heavenly Father. A lack of love in the home brings more than a third of a million couples into the divorce courts of America in an average year. Jesus explained that Moses permitted a man to divorce his wife only because he recognized the hardness and lovelessness of the human heart. "It was not what God originally intended," He told His disciples. (See Matthew 19:3-8.) A loveless home is true hell.

Love for one's country is the foundation of a nation. Without this kind of love to bind people together, everyone becomes a law unto himself, and unity and strength are dissipated. It is apparent in some nations today that a lack of love is the equivalent of the destruction of the individual spirit.

Some years ago, New York had a murder mystery which was finally solved by the arrest of several notorious criminal characters, among them a man named

31

Jack Rose. After the case was settled and the convicted criminals imprisoned, Jack Rose said something like this; "I always believed that there must be a God somewhere. But when I gave Him thought, I felt He was so far away, and so occupied with great things, that He knew nothing about me. I am sure I never would have become a criminal if the thought had ever entered my mind that God cared anything about me."

Love is the reason for God's concern about man's redemption. The Apostle John wrote, "For God so loved the world, that he gave his only begotten Son" (John 3:16, KJV). God gave because He loved. God's love for us makes us worth something. It gives us a sense of importance, a purpose in living. Life without God's love is despair.

A young Negro Puerto Rican grew up in New York City, at war within himself. His mother was a white woman, his father a dark Negro. He never knew where he belonged, he trusted no one, and his days and nights were filled with hatred and rebellion. From gang fighting he turned to narcotics. Heroin became his god, and because he had learned the power of fear early, he became a stick-up artist. It was routine for him to hold a knife against someone's throat in order to get money for drugs.

Then one day he stumbled into a little church. It was not beautiful to look at; it had cracks in the walls, but love flowed out to soften his tough heart in a way he had never known before. Through the clean bed the minister offered him, the food, the conversations with other addicts, the services which revealed Jesus Christ, and the work assignments, God's love began to heal the

32

deep gouges in his life. The love he now contains makes life not a hateful indignity to escape, but an opportunity to help others know the filling of God's Spirit.

Love is also the proof of genuine salvation. "We know we have passed from death unto life, because we love the brethren. He that loveth not his brother abideth in death" (I John 3:14, KJV). It is very plain that our love for others is a definite test of our personal salvation.

I John 3:14

This love is not cheap nor sentimental, but priceless and incomparable. The way of love is God's way, and His way is the *only* way to complete living, as well as the *best* way. Life apart from this love is sadly lacking. In fact, living without loving is merely existing.

Many will readily admit their need and even their desire to know more of God's love. The big question is, How can I know this love? Saint Paul suggests that we follow after love (see I Corinthians 14:1). The word *follow* in the original language is strenuous, not soft. This same word is used to picture Paul's relentless pursuit of the early Christians prior to his conversion. This word involves hard work, dedication, determination and sacrifice. It is the same word used by Paul when he tells us to set a goal and press on toward the prize. This prize of love can be gained only when we are willing to experience heartbreak, suffering, disappointment, frustration, exhaustion and tears. The call to love cannot be undertaken lightly. It is a full-time, lifelong vocation. Though it is not an easy road, it is a fulfilling one. Those who embark on it would not turn back for any simple pleasures of the old turned-in way of life. It is the exciting peak that must ever be climbed, the zenith of all human experience.

I COR. 14:1

A variety of signals alerted me to the supreme calling to love. Perhaps the earliest occurred when I was a student at Moody Bible Institute. An illness led to an operation which disclosed a serious tumor. My bed in Swedish Covenant Hospital became an altar as I dedicated myself to God's service. During the course of the ensuing thirty radium treatments I was told I possibly would not live long, and that even if I did it was unlikely I would ever be able to have children. This experience, along with the reading of a pamphlet on love by James McConkey, prepared me to become a living sacrifice. That was over twenty years ago, and I am not only still here and apparently healthy, but I have fathered four sons!

Some time later I was speaking in a little church in Michigan where I had been assigned a seven-day series of meetings. After the service one morning I was acutely aware that I was failing. There seemed to be no explanation for it, but nothing had gone right. After the people had left the church, I stayed behind and knelt at the front pew. As I prayed, the Lord made me painfully aware of my dishonest old self, and of my own personal, selfish ambitions. I told the Lord that I needed help—right away.

That morning, as I poured out my soul in confession, I made up my mind to pray daily for the gift of love. I vowed not to let any obstacle hinder the development of this grace within. I asked that my life become a straightforward following after love, to make this pursuit the main stream of my life, as the Apostle Paul urged. The difference in my own life has been revolutionary since love became my magnificent obsession!

Our Heavenly Father, we thank Thee for Thy great love for us. In Thy love we find purpose for living. In Thy love we find assurance of everlasting life. In Thy love we find everlasting safety. We would pray with the Apostle Paul that this love of Thine would abound in us today so that our world will be aware of our Saviour. This is our quest. In the name of Jesus Christ. Amen.

IV. LOVE IS THE GREATEST OF ALL GIFTS

IV

Love Is the Greatest
of All Gifts

Life's greatest adventure is a gift, not a
technique. St. Paul in his letter to the church at Corinth
compares love with a number of other highly prized
gifts. In every case, he points out that no matter what
else a person excels in, he is of little value unless he
possesses the greatest gift of all—love.

"Love is the medicine for the sickness of the world,"
stated Dr. Karl Menninger, one of the great contem-
porary figures in the field of medicine and psychiatry.
He instructed his staff—doctors, nurses, orderlies, and
maintenance workers—that the most important thing
they could offer any patient was love. He said that if
people can learn to give and receive love, they will
recover from their physical or emotional illnesses. A
growing number of doctors trace psychic, emotional
and physical disorders to a loveless condition in life.

Dr. Eric Berne, in his best-selling book, *Games People
Play*, discusses the tremendous need people have for en-
couragement, by word or by touch, to "keep their
spinal cords from shriveling"—to keep them alive, eager,

and confident—and talks about the variety of games people devise to win this sort of healing attention.

One man's research disclosed a shocking lack in the handling of infants some years ago. Dr. René A. Spitz was in charge of ninety-one infants in a foundling home. The babies received plenty of good food, clothing, light, air, toys, and competent care, but they lacked one indispensable thing: the attention of a mother. Each nurse cared for ten children, which gave each child the equivalent of one-tenth of a mother. The research showed that this was not enough. Three months in this home was sufficient to produce marked changes in the babies' personalities. Following up on what became of the motherless foundlings, Dr. Spitz found that 30 percent died in their first year; and twenty-one were so scarred by life they could only be classed seriously maladjusted.

It is both shocking and thrilling to realize that this world of personal love is neither sentimental nor theoretical, but shapes the very foundation of man's existence. When God told us to love Him and to love each other, He was stating the most profound principle of life itself. Our mental hospitals are full of men and women who are out of a loving relationship with other people. Intentionally or by accident, they have been hurt so badly that they have run away from the cold ordeal of living with their human associates.

How pathetically we bypass the gift of love which God holds out to us! How frequently we plant our feet firmly, and with hands on our hips, look up at God and say, "No thank You!" Our driving self-concern opposes the purpose of Almighty God. Little man cuts himself off when he refuses to love; he puts himself out of relationship with God and with others.

There is no greater gift available to man than the gift of love. When we love, God's love is released through us to others. The most concise treatise on this gift ever written is that found in Paul's first letter to his Christian brothers at Corinth, in which he contrasts and compares the gift of love (charity) with the gifts of speech, prophecy, faith, benevolence and martyrdom.

Love Is Greater Than the Ability To Speak Well

Though I speak with the tongue of men and of angels, and have not charity, I am become as sounding brass, or a tinkling cymbal [I Corinthians 13:1, KJV].

Paul discusses the gift of speech first because this was a highly prized talent in ancient Greece. Demosthenes, Sophocles, Euripides and other silver-tongued orators were the stars of that day. The Greeks were drawn to the city center where they would stand for hours, stirred by the abilities of these men. The power of persuasive speech is indeed a great gift, and throughout history masses have been moved by eloquence to heroic efforts and bloody battle. But Paul compares exciting speech without love to the tuneless crash of a cymbal, or the hollow sound of a brass gong without orchestration or melody.

It would be better never to voice sermons, speeches, conversations, anthems and hymns that are uttered without love. Christ said, "If you love me, you will keep

41

my commandments" (John 14:15, RSV). He did not tell us to multiply our prayers and praises; He told us to love: "A new commandment I give to you, that you love one another; even as I have loved you" (John 13:34, RSV).

The rapid spread of Christianity in the Roman empire was due very much to the fact that it preached the love of God by a strongly practical demonstration of love for people. The first Christians learned from Christ Himself. He showed them through His personal association with the despised and downtrodden, and His concern for the poor and afflicted, how to live a life of love. Missionary David Livingstone could not always communicate verbally with the people to whom he ministered, but these people could *feel* his love, for love has an agility that leaps over language barriers.

An inner-city youth worker I know tells the story of a young man from Harlem who spent a week with him at a high-school ranch in the Colorado Rockies. The first few days the youth was into all kinds of trouble, but by the end of the camping period he was completely won by the love of the work crew, counselors and leaders. When he returned to the city he was asked what it was that most moved him to accept Christ. His answer was, "The way people cared about me. Everybody seemed interested in what was happening to me. Nobody ever loved me like that before." As the conversation continued he told how he had heard the gospel story all his life in the ghetto, but it had meant nothing because he had never felt the love of God in his own life before.

Gina, a Chicago girl from a broken home, started

drinking wine when she was only twelve. She moved rapidly to glue sniffing, and then on to heroin. Sermons and threats were a bore to Gina, but when our church people began paying attention to her as a person, then God's love began to reach her. She could not quite get over the fact that we wanted her. When she had received our love, then she was ready to listen and understand the words that explained that God loved her too. People are just plain sick of words without love.

Love Is Greater Than Prophecy

And though I have the gift of prophecy . . .
[I Corinthians 13:2, KJV].

Webster's dictionary defines *prophecy* as the inspired declaration of divine will and purpose. What a marvelous gift this is! The prophets not only spoke forth God's truth but in many instances foretold future events. However, Paul continues to insist that wonderful as prophecy is, this gift minus love equals nothing.

The life story of Dwight L. Moody shows a simple order: first, he received grace in his life; then, there came an abandonment to the will of God. It is neither historically nor Scripturally correct to expect that an understanding of the divine will of God will create the conditions for receiving His grace. It just works the other way around, Moody said. He received his first vision of the "greatest thing in the world" during the Moorhouse meetings in 1867. For a solid week, Moorhouse preached on John 3:16. Richard Ellsworth Day, in *Bush Aglow*, gives Moody's own account of what happened to him at that meeting:

43

the MOORHOUSE meetings
1867

> I never knew up to that time that God loved us so much. This heart of mine began to thaw out; I could not keep back the tears. I just drank it in. . . . I tell you there is one thing that draws above everything else in the world and that is love.

After this happened, Moody, who was already a pastor, saw for the first time the secret of a winsome church:

> The churches would soon be filled, if outsiders could find that people in them loved them when they came. This love draws sinners! We must win them to us first, then we can win them to Christ. We must get the people to love us, and then turn them over to Christ.

Matthew recounts Christ's painting a picture of one, who perhaps had his order reversed, calling in the judgment day, "Lord, have we not prophesied in thy name?" (7:22, KJV). The answer is, "I never knew you: depart from me, ye that work iniquity" (v. 23). Love is greater than prophecy, and must precede it.

. . . and understand all mysteries . . . [I Corinthians 13:2, KJV].

Here Paul speaks of divine insight concerning hidden truths. In my travels and my reading, I have met spiritual giants, who challenged me to greater living. Other times I have been keenly disappointed to find people more concerned about hidden mysteries than about needy people. That's a paradox, isn't it? But it's a common one. Too often Christians are concerned about hidden truth, but indifferent about loving difficult people. Skill

44

in unraveling the mysteries of God is very desirable and important, yet this without love for people equals nothing.

It is one thing to know that love is the conquering weapon, the greatest gift. But it is quite another thing to secure it. Moody's account, quoted in *Bush Aglow*, tells how Moorhouse went on to show him that love comes first when we find out exactly what the Bible *says*:

> I took up that word Love, and I do not know how many weeks I spent in studying the passages in which it occurs, *till at last I could not help loving people.* I had been feeding on Love so long that I was anxious to do everybody good I came in contact with.
>
> I got full of it. It ran out my fingers. You take up the subject of love in the Bible! You will get so full of it that all you have got to do is to open your lips, and a flood of the Love of God flows out. . . .

Love Is Greater Than Knowledge

. . . and all knowledge . . . [v. 2].

Knowledge is a rare gem, and we would never handle this expensive jewel carelessly. Yet there is nothing so hard and cold as knowledge without love.

Moody was miserable before he felt the power of God's love in his life and his ministry. His congregations showed signs of falling away. He found himself wondering if the gospel might not need something else to make it attractive to people. While riding on a train from California, where he had attended a Sunday-school convention, he recalled young Moorhouse saying to him, four years earlier:

45

You are sailing on the wrong track. If you will
change your course, and learn to preach *God's words*
instead of your own, He will make you a great power.

Moody had realized then that he had been desperately
trying to explain what the Bible *teaches* before filling his
soul with what it *says*. When Moorhouse had left Chicago, Moody had not followed the new light; he had
taken a course of reading. And when he selected a text
and started to preach, he immediately departed from it.
Now, sitting on the train, he recalled with new meaning
what an old gentleman in Boston had told him years
before: "Young man, when you speak again, honor the
Holy Ghost."

That summer Moody made the rewarding committal
of giving even his ignorance to Christ, and new life
flooded his church. Even the heat of August didn't keep
the people away. Moody realized humbly that power
was present now—power that had never been there in
the parade of his own knowledge.

Love ignores high-sounding explanations and goes to
work. Love gets us in gear with God and the times. Love
transforms our doctrine into power. Love adds feet to
facts, resulting in action. The need of this hour, as much
as Moody's, is for the marriage of love to knowledge.

Moody's sound advice to his successor was this:
"Dr. Erdman, give the people the importance of love.
If they are right here, they will be right 95 percent of
the time."

A churchwoman once confessed to me, "I have been
a Christian for twenty years now. During that time I
have read many books on winning others, yet I do not

46

know of anyone that I have led to the Lord. I have memorized Scripture and know how to meet the objections of the unconverted, but still I have brought no one to a decision. Why have I been so useless?"

My answer caused surprise. "You are a fruitless Christian," I told her, "because your eyes are dry."

"I don't understand," she said, and so I added, "You have failed not for want of knowledge but for lack of love for people. 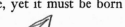When you really love someone, you will weep for them."

This lady returned home to read the Scriptures and to pray. As she prayed, her heart became strangely warmed. Her unbelieving sister came vividly to her mind, she got up from her knees to find her, and with genuine tears threw her arms around her sister and admitted in love, "More than anything in this world, I want you to be a Christian!" They came together to the meeting that night, and when I gave an invitation the two of them walked up together to respond to the appeal.

Is it our rapidly increasing bookishness that makes us so tactful that we become fearful of trying to make contact? Are we more concerned about what people think, than about what God thinks? Paul went even farther when he wrote, ". . . I could wish that myself were accursed from Christ for my brethren, my kinsmen according to the flesh" (Romans 9:3, KJV). That is shocking! What is he saying? He is expressing his willingness to be forever damned if that would save others. What a staggering illustration of love! This is a redemptive love very few of us know much about. Knowledge is extremely important, especially in our age, yet it must be born in love to be eternal.

ROMANS
9:3

One day some years ago I went to visit a man who was called the roughest man in town. As I attempted to share my knowledge of God with him, he cursed the church, the Bible and me. Then he threatened to throw me out bodily if I ever returned to his home again. As I made my watchful retreat, I said quietly, "Mr. Baldwin, God loves you and I love you." I was not prepared for what happened. Almost instantly he melted. He slipped to his knees and wept uncontrollably as he emptied out a heart full of hatred and sin. It was God's love that did it. That rough railroader was gloriously changed by the gospel. Knowledge without love is impotent, but together they generate tremendous force.

Love Is Greater Than Faith

. . . *and if I have all faith, so as to remove mountains, and have not love, I am nothing* [I Corinthians 13:2, RSV].

The faith referred to here is that of working wonders. Faith is a great gift. In fact, without faith we cannot please God. An individual must come to Christ and rest in Him before he can know anything of God's love.

An exciting breakthrough came to a group of New England pastors who met in Boston for three days in a fellowship of love that ignited their faith. One of the men who attended said, "We listened, learned, and loved. We were reconciled and brought together! The world will never really believe in the power of Christ until it can see us one in love and appreciation, respecting each other as men, attempting to discover ever more clearly the features of the Risen Christ. . . .

"The world is a place of haunted men. They are in

agony in the midst of splendor. The ache for integrity, for reconciliation, for oneness is gnawing them into a state of stupefaction. Every human being is like a house. There is only one key for all houses: Jesus. You and I have that key; if we do not work together to bring that key to every house in the world, then we are the murderers of the world" (*Faith at Work*, April, 1964). Without the love of Christ nourishing our behavior, we bring the powerlessness of a dead faith to a dying world.

Paul writes, "And I pray that Christ will be more and more at home in your hearts, living within you as you trust in Him. May your roots go down deep into the soil of God's marvelous love" (Ephesians 3:17). Paul was so emphatically the Apostle of faith that his conclusion is all the more revealing. Faith is great, but love is greater. Faith has priority, but love has preeminence. Faith is first, but love is last. Faith connects the soul with God, and God is love. Faith is the means that God uses to bring us into His love, but faith without love places us in life's minus column!

Love Is Greater Than Benevolence

And though I bestow all my goods to feed the poor, and though I give my body to be burned, and have not charity, it profiteth me nothing [I Corinthians 13:3, KJV].

All of us have given to help the poor: a dinner to the hungry, a donation to the underprivileged, a dollar to the cripple as he stretches out his tin cup. Prosperity imposes the obligation to help those who have not. The needy are all about us, but often benevolence is an act of relief for a guilty conscience. It is too easy in our prosperous times to write a check and dismiss our responsibility for caring. Even the emperors of Rome gave lavishly on special holidays to keep the masses under their control, but they gave without loving. How humiliating would be a revelation of the motives for our own deeds!

The pattern of life in the early church indicates a joint method of taking care of people. Those first Christians had learned from Christ that it was impossible to belong to each other and yet be indifferent to the needs of a member. The phrase used in Acts, "in common," seems to indicate their belief that God's gifts were meant to supply the needs of all, and should be shared with others. What was not essential for their own needs was shared with the poor. As Bernard F. Meyer says, "We cannot but think that He often invited the poor to eat with Him, rather than giving them a backdoor handout."

This quality of giving can only spring from love. It is neither an action pasted on to satisfy a requirement, nor an excuse to buy our way free from personal involvement. The love which is already present within us, because God is there, bears fruit in our sharing our resources gladly. On the other hand, the Pharisees sounded the trumpets so that everyone would notice they were giving. The Bible says, "They have their reward" (Mathew 6:2, KJV). It is not so much what we give, but how we give it. *We can give without loving, but we cannot love without giving.* Love is greater than any act of benevolence.

Love Is Greater Than Martyrdom

. . . and though I give my body to be burned, and have

not charity, it profiteth me nothing [I Corinthians 13:3 KJV].

Martyrdom is farther from our experience today than it was at the time Paul was writing to the Corinthians. Undoubtedly there were Christians in Corinth who suffered the fiery faggots and the lions' teeth. In those days hundreds endured physical violence because of their deep love for Christ. This text suggests, however, that martyrdom could result from something other than consecration. Perhaps it could be fanatical devotion to a cause, rather than love for Christ. Martyrdom may be more out of principle than out of love.

The war in Vietnam has produced some spectacular instances of martyrdom, such as the young man who set fire to himself in Washington and burned to death in protest as people watched helplessly. The Buddhist monks who became fiery pillars to a pacifist principle were modern-day martyrs for a cause.

A generation ago there was a common plea for young people to love Christ enough to *die* for Him. Today the plea more commonly assumes that it takes as much or more courage to *live* for Him. To live a life in relationship to those around us is no easy calling. It calls for every ounce of commitment we can uncover. Living the love of God is the greatest challenge, the highest calling to which a human being can respond. Someone once said, "Love is appealing, but its practice is appallingly difficult."

We humans are crafty creatures who rationalize so much that it is difficult to decide what our real motives are. Will you try an experiment? Stop reading right now. Look over your life. Analyze your failures, your restless spirit, your dissatisfaction. You will probably discover that love is the missing link. Certainly a portion of the good news of the gospel lies in the difference Christ promised us as we come to Him. We need to heed the advice of Scripture, ". . . seek ye first the kingdom of God, and his righteousness; and all these things shall be added unto you" (Matthew 6:33, KJV).

John Calvin, commenting on these verses, said, "For where love is wanting, the beauty of all virtue is mere tinsel, is empty sound, is not worth a straw, nay more, is offensive and disgusting."

Life with all its gifts, minus love, equals zero.

> *Lord, Thy love is greater than all the gifts of the Spirit. Take my lips and talk through them; take my mind and think through it; take my knowledge and set it on fire; take my heart and flood it with Thy love. Dear Lord, love this world through me. Amen.*

V. THE COLORS OF LOVE

V

The Colors of Love

As the artist combines colors to produce a masterpiece, so the Bible reveals many characteristics which, blended together, give a beautiful portrait of Jesus Christ. From Bethlehem's manger to the mount of Ascension, the life of Christ was a life of unselfish love. Every characteristic of love is not only fulfilled in Christ, but the achievement of these same characteristics should be the goal of every Christian.

Love is very patient and kind . . . [I Corinthians 13:4].

There is no doubt that people are always hungry for kindness. Kindness might be defined as the expression of a friendly, sympathetic nature. Goethe penned, "Kindness is the golden chain by which society is bound together." There are times when we suffer long, but are we kind?

A pastor in Pennsylvania discovered two women living in the neighborhood of his church. He sensed that they were not only lonely, but in need of help. Rumors of their odd behavior led him to select one of his parishioners who had an extra measure of courage and kindness. Even she, however, felt apprehensive as she walked up the path to the run-down house.

The door was opened only a crack in response to her knock, but after she blurted out that the pastor who had called the day before had sent her, she was admitted. The house was dark; all the shades were drawn.

The woman who had fearfully opened the door led the way to a bedroom where her mother lay, frowning and suspicious. The daughter's rambling explanations reminded the visitor of the vague reports she had heard from neighbors about "violent days." Fear sprang up in her heart, but it gave way to unusual kindness and love as she began to concentrate on the thought, "God loves you and I love you." What a change she felt come over her as she began to really listen, without fear of what the woman might do to her! Before leaving the house she even put her arms around the big, straggly-haired woman and gave her a hug and a kiss. Tears came to the woman's eyes, and she held the visitor a long time. Here was the kindness of Christ reaching out to someone starved for love; and it opened the way to a new adventure for a number of people.

Two families donated coal to heat the house; another gave a refrigerator; some contributed clothes; the church made a television set available; the elderly mother was given badly needed hospital care. Children made cards and cookies. One man began to take care of the women's lawn. A neighbor offered the use of her telephone whenever needed. Another woman took time regularly to drive the daughter to the market for groceries.

Eventually the new friendships began to include a rather timid time of praying together, with tears of love and joy and thankfulness shining in all eyes. Then they moved into reading the New Testament, and discussed several verses before praying. Eventually a decision was made to receive Jesus Christ.

The difference then and now is apparent in many ways—even in little things. The woman who first showed kindness says, "We had invited the daughter to join us one evening. What a change from the bedraggled, sullen, unhappy person I had first met! She was wearing her best dress; her hair was attractively arranged. Now she had reason to feel like getting dressed up!"

What a privilege it is just to be able to get into a car and drive somewhere! Yet how rarely do we ever think of extending such an ordinary kindness. For people like this lonely woman, a simple invitation to ride along becomes an occasion!

When the visits to this home first began the women often asked, "Why do you care? Why do you come?" And the reply was always the same: "Because God loves you, and I love you." What an evidence of the indwelling presence of Jesus Christ we can present when we express to others the warm loving-kindness that is characteristic of our Saviour.

Love is kind even when misunderstood and falsely accused. Love knows how to take sorrow and heartache cheerfully. The verb for *is kind* implies active service. Our old flesh is hasty, hotheaded and unkind, but divine love is very different.

Some years ago I was misunderstood and criticized by people who I expected would know better. I desperately wanted to retaliate, or at least present my version of the story. By bulldog determination, I clenched my fist, bit my lip, and actually managed to keep my mouth shut. But I surely was not gracious, and I didn't display much kindness.

Christ spent His life seeking to make others happy. For thirty-three years He went about doing kind deeds, ministering to the sick, feeding the hungry, comforting the bereaved and even performing a miracle at a wedding feast. Jesus was kind.

Our Saviour was long-suffering with His weak-willed disciples who disappointed Him so often. He was merciful to the despised and the mentally disturbed. He was long-suffering with Pilate, with the Roman centurion, with the crucified thief. Our Saviour suffered long and was kind in His dying hours. After the nails had done their ugly work He cried out, saying, "Father, forgive them; for they know not what they do" (Luke 23:34, KJV).

This love goes beyond understanding; yet this is the kind of love God would manifest through us. Stephen amid the stones prayed, "Lord, lay not this sin to their charge" (Act 7:60, KJV). What kind of love is this? It is a constancy of love amid neglect, ignorance, lack of appreciation, and even undeserved violence. Why can love endure? Because God is sovereign and everything belongs to Him. He gives us the capacity to live victoriously. Someone has changed the words of the hymn "Are Ye Able" to read this way:

Able to suffer without complaining;
To be misunderstood without explaining;

Able to give without receiving,
To be ignored without grieving;

58

Able to ask without commanding,
To love despite misunderstanding;

Able to turn to the Lord for guarding;
Able to wait for His own rewarding.

A love that suffers long, and is kind, is power beyond our comprehension or capacity. The entire Bible is an illustration of God's long-suffering to mankind. With monotonous repetition the Israelites murmured against and even forsook Jehovah, yet He suffered long and was kind.

I once heard a father say to a friend who was having disciplinary problems with his son, "You know, we can't always be in the good graces of our children. Sometimes we have to be willing to be just an old doormat, and let them walk all over us—or be an old tyrant, and say 'No.' "

What he meant in this case was another example of the need for long-suffering as a characteristic of genuine love. Sometimes a parent may be tempted to go along with what a child requests, because it will make the child happy and easier to live with. But the course of love may have to take the unpleasant, long-suffering route which sees further than a child can see. It may need to say a firm "yes" or a firm "no" and to stick to an unwelcome course of action, regardless of the complaining, the tears, the foot stompings, the tantrums, the indignation, even the hatred, on the part of the child.

Do you recall the fable about two mountain goats approaching one another on a narrow ledge? Realizing there was no room to pass, they reared and bucked, but neither budged. They backed up, charged, and locked horns again, but each held his ground. Again they parted and charged; then like Gibraltar they stood unmovable. Finally the sensible one knelt down, and let the other one climb over him. Then they both went merrily on their way. Sometimes we too must let people walk over us. Love is magnanimous.

Love is . . . never jealous or envious . . . [I Corinthians 13:4].

Jealousy caused Joseph to be sold into Egypt; his half-brothers were discontented because he was the favored son of Jacob. Cain's envy made him a murderer. Envy showed in the attitude of the elder brother in the story of the Prodigal Son. When he heard the rejoicing over his wayward brother, the Scripture says, ". . . he was angry and would not go in" (Luke 15:28, KJV). Both brothers missed the father's love—one because he was a prodigal, and the other because he was envious. Envy is essentially satanic wherever it appears.

Envy exists in almost everyone. It is a disease that disturbs the mind and consumes the body. Some people become physically ill because of envy.

The Book of Proverbs declares, "A sound heart is the life of the flesh: but envy the rottenness of the bones" (14:30, KJV). Envy keeps no holidays, but works continually. Envy is discontentment at the good fortunes of others. Envy says, "I cannot eat, and therefore want all others to starve. If I cannot see in one eye, I want you to be blind in both eyes."

According to James, jealousy is a characteristic of earthly wisdom which results in confusion and disorder and all kinds of evil: "And by all means don't brag about being wise and good if you are bitter and jealous and selfish; that is the worst sort of lie. For jealousy and selfishness are not God's kind of wisdom. Such things are earthly, unspiritual, inspired by the devil, and come from hell itself. For wherever there is jealousy or selfish ambition, there will be disorder and every other kind of evil" (James 3:14-16).

King Saul envied David to such a degree that he lost control of his faculties. Envy is usually a trait of the carnal or unregenerate soul. In contrast, love rejoices when others excel. Jonathan, Saul's son, could have been afflicted with the same satanic disease as his father; but he dethroned envy with love. ". . . he loved him [David] as he loved his own soul" (I Samuel 20:17, KJV).

A good way to cure envy is to pray sincerely for the one of whom you are envious. Paul plainly tells us, "For the whole Law can be summed up in this one command: 'Love others as you love yourself.' But if instead of showing love among yourselves you are always critical and catty, watch out! Beware of ruining each other" (Galatians 5:14-15).

The Christians at the church of Corinth were immature too. "For you are still only baby Christians, controlled by your own desires, not God's. When you are jealous of one another and divide up into quarreling groups, doesn't that prove you are still babies, wanting your own way? In fact, you are acting like people who don't belong to the Lord at all" (I Corinthians 3:3).

The event of falling in love is one of the sweetest universal experiences of humanity. We all know the strong sweep of outgoing feeling which leads us to forget ourselves and to promise a beloved one anything. We meet

61

someone who helps us leap over the walls of our own selfhood. We come out of our own concern and are caught up with the well-being of another. Without expecting it, or working towards it, we spontaneously and magnificently fulfill the law of God (towards one person!) by loving someone else as much as we do ourselves!

This is a spectacular happening! There is no desire or temptation to "puff" ourselves. Our only concern is to build up the beloved. Our pride in her company, her attention, her abilities is radiant, and everyone recognizes it in our behavior. The hitch arises when we discover after a week, or a month, or a year that this high and lofty condition is temporary, or at best intermittent. The old self, which we thought we had set aside in our love for another, rears up and starts begging for attention, for flattery, for recognition. Only as our human love bows before the love of God and invites His humility and His grace into the experience, can it become a dependable and lasting love that is not proud of its own abilities.

In one of Aesop's fables, a fly sat upon the axle of a chariot wheel and said, "What a dust do I raise!" Empty trucks always make the most noise. The proud have an exaggerated idea of their own importance. Their primary interest is in the first person.

Pride is often at the bottom of our biggest blunders. A young Scottish minister once stepped into the pulpit with pride and complete self-confidence, but his sermon acted on the congregation like a double dose of sleeping pills. The message was a failure, and he knew it. As he left the pulpit in defeat an old lady whispered, "Son, if you had gone up the way you came down, you would have come down the way you went up!" Love is humble. It does not boast about itself.

When a committee from Jerusalem asked John the Baptist if he were the Messiah, he answered them " 'I am not. . . .' '. . . then, who are you?' " John said, "I am a voice . . ." (John 1:19-23). He plainly told them that he was not the way, but just the way-shower.

John stood with two of his disciples, and he said, "Behold the Lamb of God! And the two disciples heard him speak, and they followed Jesus" (John 1:36, KJV). John was so filled with love for Jesus that self-conscious pride was impossible.

Love does not parade for the applause of the crowd but places itself below all others. God keeps His best gifts on the lower shelves. Humility precedes honor as "an haughty spirit before a fall" (Proverbs 16:18, KJV). The Apostle Paul said, "Knowledge puffeth up, but love edifieth" (I Corinthians 8:1, KJV). The word *puff* is defined as any sudden or short blast of wind. The love of Christ is not sudden or brief; it is eternal. Love builds forever.

A missionary once was translating the word *pride*. To properly convey the meaning she wrote, "the ears are too far apart." Pride was simply an inflated head. Love is not big-headed; it is big-hearted. The greater a person's ability, the less boasting he needs to do; and conversely, the less ability one has, the more noise he has to make about it. Love sees ourselves as we really are in the sight of God.

63

Heavenly Father, I thank Thee for the power and patience of love. Give me a heart that need not boast, and a spirit that is kind. Let me walk in the fullness of Thy love this day. Make me to be like Jesus Christ. Amen.

VI. LOVE AND CONDUCT

VI

Love and Conduct

In a sophisticated civilization such as ours, here in the mid-twentieth century, we think of our conduct as a pretty highly polished way of life. We observe the rules for etiquette, congratulate our friends in their promotions, play it cool when we're crossed so we don't appear ruffled by all the idiots around us, and smooth over the weaknesses of our loved ones. We smile at people we dislike and exchange greetings with our enemies, invite the new neighbors in for coffee and give Thanksgiving baskets to the poor family on the other side of the tracks, and then pat ourselves on the back for being downright friendly folks!

The "charity" that the Apostle Paul is talking about in his discussion of human behavior is a considerably more difficult way of life.

Love . . . is {not} selfish nor rude [I Corinthians 13:5].

We know it is the polite thing for a man to stand when a woman enters the room; to say "thank you" for a gift. We know that a gentleman removes his hat upon entering a house, and that well-bred children hop up to offer their seats to adults coming into the room. But many of these things we do merely out of a feeling of

67

social responsibility. And sometimes we wish we didn't have to do them. They become a chore, a duty, and there is little joy in the gesture.

What a difference when we truly love someone! How we jump to do the little things that are signals of our loving attention! True courtesy is love in action in society. I have heard politeness defined as love in trifles. To do little things for others, in a way that is genuine, is to prove one's love. Even the most uncultured person can go into a foreign situation and behave politely, if he is a person who has a reservoir of love in his heart. Love just does not behave in a discourteous manner. Greed does; selfishness does; fear does—but not love.

Analyze yourself the next time you get delayed in a traffic jam and lean on the horn. Check up on what's wrong inside of you when you hurry past that woman with the overloaded shopping cart to get to the cash register first with your bread and milk and hamburger. What is pushing you? Courtesy does not push other people around; love expresses itself by making the way easier for someone. It kneels to serve another.

I once knew a husband who had entered into a new relationship with Christ, and wanted to share it with his wife. Years before he had decided that one chore he would not do around the house was carry out the garbage—he would do anything else gladly, but not that. Now, as he began asking the Lord how he could get through to his wife, there seemed to be no approach that was not prefaced by that garbage sack sitting by the back door. So finally he stooped down, picked the bag up, and carried it out to the alley. His love for both God and his wife had grown past the point where he had to prove his superiority. He was free to become a garbage carrier in love.

The one who allows the love of Christ to control him is not hard or harsh, crude or rude, rough or tough. He is gentle and courteous. While the word *courteous* originaly came from *court* and suggested the manners which prevailed in the palaces of kings and queens, eventually it came to mean consideration for others. Paul suggests this rule: ". . . let each esteem other [or others] better than themselves" (Philippians 2:3, KJV). A. T. Williams translates it, "Stop acting from motives of selfish strife or petty ambition, but in humility practice treating one another as your superiors." John Donne wrote, "No man is an island, entire of itself, every man is a piece of the continent." One of the proofs of our love is the helping hand we hold out to a needy world— beginning under our very own roof.

Courtesy springs from love as the spring flowers from the fertile soil in the woods. Regardless of background, a Christian man will become a gentleman and a Christian woman, a lady. Why? Because when God's love is planted in us we grow to be like Christ. Love transforms the commonest of mortals.

We live in a world that toots its own horn. We seem to be taught from the time we grab the blocks away from a playmate, that we can shove a little bit here, and pull a little bit there, and somehow come out on top. "One-upmanship" is the game of the day. "Get ahead," the world says; "step on anybody you like as you climb to the top." Whether we are heading for the presidency of the PTA, or the manager's spot in our department, almost subconscious schemes form in our brains as we figure out how we can make ourselves look better than Sally or Joe. We tell ourselves that if we do not push ourselves forward and use others to further our own goals, we may be scoffed at as shiftless victims of inferiority complexes who just can't make the grade. How completely different from God's approach!

Manhattan Project Number Two is the story of a man who had to learn to be a servant for Christ's sake. Red Cap 42 carried people's bags for forty years. He was so disgusted with his role in life that whenever anyone asked him his occupation he would say he was "in the leather business." He hated everybody because having to carry others' baggage made him feel he was not as good as they were.

After Christ came into his life, Red Cap 42's whole outlook changed, even though he stayed in the same business, he was carrying bags for God now, and he began talking with God all the time about his customers. Person after person sensed this elderly Negro's attitude. Many came into a personal relationship with the Saviour through the witness of this Red Cap, Ralston Young. They began to meet together with him for prayer in an empty railroad coach parked on a siding.

Presently a group of these businessmen rented an office for Ralston Young on New York's Madison Avenue, where they could have regular prayer meetings. They formed a board and since the atomic bomb had been Manhattan Project Number One, they named their prayer project, Manhattan Project Number Two. God had used Ralston Young greatly in his position as a bag carrier. Now he has an office of his own and even a secretary—his wife. As Ralston Young explained, "I have

v.5

to have a secretary because I can't read and write. But my wife can. She writes the letters for me."

Love seeketh not her own [I Corinthians 13:5, KJV].

Love does not push itself into the limelight. Love does not strive for place or position. In God's program, we stoop to conquer; we kneel to rise. The way up is the way down. The secret is the surrendering of our will to the will of God, so that His way becomes our way. Andrew Murray said, "Do you want to enter what people call 'the higher life'? Then go a step lower down."

Joseph of the Old Testament went down into the pit, down into the slavery, down into the dungeon for thirteen years; then, because he had done his work well and faithfully he was lifted up and eventually became ruler of all Egypt. We must go down before we go up; we must go deeper before we go farther. Love walks softly and seeks not her own way. The greatest happiness in life comes from giving, not from getting. "Bear ye one another's burdens, and so fulfil the law of Christ" (Galatians 6:2, KJV). The Bible indicates that one of the signs of the end times is selfishness. "This know also, that in the last days perilous times shall come. For men shall be lovers of their own selves, covetous, boasters, proud, blasphemers, disobedient to parents, unthankful, unholy" (II Timothy 3:1-2, KJV).

v.5

Love is not irritable or touchy [I Corinthians 13:5].

Irritability is one of the products of our nervous atomic space age. We rush here and there; we don't know where we're going, but we're already ten minutes late. I am amused when I watch shoppers in a department store get excited because they missed one section of a revolving door. The center of irritability is self. The test of your spirituality is not measured at the Sunday worship service, but at home when your son kicks his pajamas under the bed instead of placing them in the hamper, or when the coats are hung on the floor instead of in the closet. The validity of faith is not discovered at the Lord's Table on Sunday, but at the breakfast table on Monday. We entertain the stranger with smiles, while our loved ones are hurt by neglect and familarity. The toughest place for love is at home. Paul writes that love is not provoked. The word *easily* is often seized as an excuse for letting off steam, but this word is not found in any of the original manuscripts. Probably some of the translators in 1611 thought Paul was going a bit too far, so they added the word *easily* to *The King James Version!*

I know of a little boy who went riding with his daddy. The father drove with little regard for anyone. He fussed and fumed, bellowed and shouted as he drove through town. Finally, they arrived home. Later that same day the boy was out in the car with his mother. As they drove peacefully along, the boy said, "Mom, where are all the idiots?"

"Idiots?" exclaimed the mother.

"Yes, this morning when I was out with daddy, we met seven of them!"

Love is the best ointment for irritability, right where we live. This sin has spoiled the peace of many homes. Some people are harder to get along with than a bale of barbed wire.

There is a tradition that Jonathan Edwards, third

president of Princeton and one of America's great preachers, had a daughter with an ungovernable temper. But, as is often the case, this failing was not known to the outside world. A young man fell in love with this daughter and asked to marry her.

"You can't have her," was the abrupt answer of Jonathan Edwards.

"But I love her," the young man replied.

"You can't have her," repeated Edwards.

"But she loves me," replied the young man.

Again Edwards said, "You can't have her."

"Why?" asked the young man.

"Because she is not worthy of you."

"But," he asked, "she is Christian, is she not?"

"Yes, she is a Christian, but the grace of God can live with some people with whom no one else could ever live!"

The secret of the temper is more than self-control; it is Christ-control. All of us have dynamite in the cellar, and whenever we walk without God and the power of His love, we must expect explosions.

A woman said to her pastor, "I lose my temper, but it's all over in a minute." The pastor answered, "And so is the atom bomb. But think of the damage it produces!" When you lose control of yourself in any way, you really lose the ability to think and act as a rational human being. You become in a sense subhuman.

"A wholesome tongue is a tree of life: but perverseness therein is a breach in the spirit" (Proverbs 15:4, KJV). "God's people must not be quarrelsome; they must be gentle, patient teachers of those who are wrong" (II Timothy 2:24).

73

Henry Drummond spoke about temper in his address, "The Greatest Thing in the World": "It is the intermittent fever which bespeaks unintermittent disease within; the occasional bubble escaping to the surface which betrays some rottenness underneath; a sample of the most hidden products of the soul dropped involuntarily when off one's guard; in a word, the lightning form of a hundred hideous and unchristian sins. A want of patience, a want of kindness, a want of generosity, a want of courtesy, a want of unselfishness, are all instantaneously symbolized in one flash of temper.

"Hence it is not enough to deal with the temper. We must go to the source and change the inmost nature. . . . Souls are made sweet not by taking the acid fluids out but by putting something in—a great love, a new spirit, the Spirit of Christ. . . . This only can eradicate what is wrong, work a chemical change, renovate . . . the inner man."

It does not hold grudges and will hardly even notice when others do it wrong [I Corinthians 13:5].

Love is optimistic; it looks at people in the best light. Love thinks constructively as it senses the grand possibilities in other people. What a delightful condition to live in! How warming and vigorating to step into the brightness of this kind of love, even for a few minutes! Everyone has an inner longing to feel important, to do something unique, to have an assurance of one's own worth. Young people particularly have a terrible self-image. Their sense that they are not worth very much makes suicide rank in fifth place among the causes of adolescent death.

74

There's a preacher in New Jersey who has turned in his pulpit for a lunch counter across from the high school. For seven years he had been concerned about the people who never came inside his church. The first seven months after he bought the luncheonette he made more contacts among teen-agers than in the seven previous years! He uses the interview technique at the counter, and carefully records each answer given him by a boy or girl. Then, during a conversation which arises around the significant questions he has asked, he hands his customer a little book. They usually read it and come back. They feel trusted. Bill Iverson says, "Teen-agers want strong adult authority figures and adults who will listen to them, as well as acceptance by their peer group. They are crying for adults whom they can respect and who will tell them what to do at the right time . . . teen-agers aren't asking for perfection—just honesty and integrity—what any adult ought to be able to give."

God has called us to be the expression of His love among the people of our own private world. If we can contain His kind of love that reaches out to others and holds no grudges, we will truly be light to brighten dark lives, for Christ's sake.

Dr. George W. Crane, author and social psychologist, has written a pamphlet called "The Compliment Club" (available from The Hopkins Syndicate, Mellot, Indiana). To qualify for membership in this club, a person undertakes to pay three sincere compliments a day, one to each of three different persons, for a month. He is encouraged to pay these to even casual contacts or complete strangers. The doctor points out that love cannot replace dislike or indifference at a moment's notice; it requires development of a definite technique, and of skill in approaching people.

Love grows through the showing of appreciation and dies without it. Christians ought to be the most skilled social detectives, ferreting out the good points in our associates. "You can sincerely compliment your worst enemy, for no human being is totally lacking in merits," says Dr. Crane.

He tells many stories of how paying compliments changed people's lives. One woman working in a millinery house thought that Laura, who worked across the room from her, was snobbish and aloof. One day, however, to fill her quota of compliments, she said, "Laura, do you know that every time I glance up I see your head silhouetted against the window? I think you have the prettiest profile and hair of anyone I know."

Laura looked up startled, then began to cry. "That's the first kind word anybody has said to me in all the seventeen years I have worked here." All that time she had been hiding her loneliness from her co-workers behind a pseudo-sophistication.

"Friendship," says Dr. Crane, "is a flower. To obtain a lovely flower, somebody must do the work of planting the seed, watering and cultivating it."

Isn't this what Christ did? When He stopped to ask water from the Samaritan woman, when He told Zacchaeus He was going home to dinner with him, He was implying a compliment. He did somewhat the same thing with the despised publicans and sinners, even when He accepted the invitations of the Pharisees. What an important part of Christian love this is—to look for the good in people and help them to recognize it; to let them know that you believe good of them, rather than evil.

Abraham Lincoln once said, "The best way to destroy your enemy is to make him your friend."

On a very intimate level we can gain another truth from this phrase about love. "Think no evil" is the *King James* translation. Love casts out the evil thinking that spoils our daydreams and our quiet times. Thoughts are the seeds to future deeds. God can not only cleanse the soul and heal the body; He can also purify the mind. Believers who would never dream of doing evil sometimes in their thinking wander down sordid paths. You become what you think.

A young man, emerging from an evil place, accidentally met his pastor on the street. "I'm sorry," said the young man, "I had no business being there."

The wise pastor jolted the young man as he said, "When you came out and I saw you, you lost only your reputation. When you went in, and only God saw you, you lost your character."

Thousands of people have good reputations but have lost their characters. All-knowing God knows our thoughts completely.

Paul begs Christians to bring "into captivity every thought to the obedience of Christ" (II Corinthians 10:5, KJV). Yes, God cleanses the mind as He pours in His love. A university student approached me after a lecture and said, "I'm a Christian, but I'm up and down. My life is not consistent or constant." I made arrangements to meet him and further discuss his dilemma. When we met, I suggested going to his room. His definite reluctance was so obvious that I was sure my visit to his room would reveal his problem. With his permission, we entered. I scanned the room with its pictures and books and immediately knew his trouble. Though upright in his conduct, the young man was filling his mind with the stories from pulp magazines and suggestive pictures. No wonder he was up and down in his experience! I counseled with him about his problem, and I am happy to say that after graduating from the university he went on to seminary, and today has his own pastorate. The Scriptures can fill up the mind with life and hope. The love of Christ flows into the hungry places of our minds and souls and nourishes them abundantly. In this sense too, love thinks no evil.

It is interesting to notice that Paul tells the Philippians to think positively about wholesome virtues: ". . . whatsoever things are true, whatsoever things are honest, whatsoever things are just, whatsoever things are pure, whatsoever things are lovely, whatsoever things are of good report; if there be any virtue, and if there be any praise, think on these things" (Philippians 4:8, KJV). The phrase, "think on these things," means take an inventory of these things. Love notices and concentrates upon honesty, justice, purity, loveliness, and goodness, but not evil.

One man who began to allow love to come through in his daily contacts with people said, "I have found that the world is filled with interesting people. I just never realized it before." When the love of God leads us to see new values in others, we lose ourselves. And when we lose ourselves, as the Bible so paradoxically tells us, we finally begin to find ourselves!

All of this wonderful new kind of life, of course, is

impractical and impossible apart from the indwelling Holy Spirit. The Holy Spirit is the One who loves spontaneously. With Him inside us, we begin to love as Christ loved. But He cannot work unless we allow Him to pour Himself through our thoughts and our actions. Start with the first person you meet in the day. Is it your wife? your husband? the elevator operator? the bus driver? the paper boy? Maybe you are not in the habit of saying anything beyond a sort of unintelligible growl. Look at this person in a whole new way— here is someone God's love can touch through you. Put yourself in the other person's shoes a minute, and see what comment you can make, what question you can phrase, that will make him feel good, make him know someone really cares.

On the other hand, if you don't really care, you can just go on using the same old recipe for a miserable life:

Think about yourself.

Talk about yourself.

Use *I* as often as possible.

Mirror yourself continually in the opinion of others.

Listen greedily to what people say about you.

Expect to be appreciated.

Be suspicious.

Be jealous and envious.

Be sensitive to slights.

Never forgive a criticism.

Trust nobody but yourself.

Insist on consideration and respect.

Demand agreement with your own views on everything.

Sulk if people are not grateful to you for favors shown them.

Never forget a service you may have rendered.
Be on the lookout for a good time for yourself.
Shirk your duties if you can.
Do as little as possible for others.
Love yourself supremely.
Be selfish.

I am assured that this recipe is guaranteed to make one miserable! Love, on the contrary, never acts in any of these ways. "Now you can have real love for everyone because your souls have been cleansed from selfishness and hatred when you trusted Christ to save you; so see to it that you really do love each other warmly, with all your hearts" (I Peter 1:22).

Heavenly Father, this is our earnest prayer. May Thy love in us be felt by others. ". . . we will lovingly follow the truth at all times—speaking truly, dealing truly, living truly—and so become more and more in every way like Christ who is the head of His body, the church. Under His direction the whole body is fitted together perfectly, and each part in its own special way helps the other parts, so that the whole body is healthy and growing and full of love" (Ephesians 4:15, 16). Amen.

VII. LOVE ONE ANOTHER

VII

Love One Another

People are little different today than they were in Christ's day. Human beings need to see and touch and feel in order to understand love. So God expressed His love centuries ago in a familiar form, one that could be seen and heard and experienced—Jesus Christ. Today He still requires people to be Christlike, so the modern world too can feel His love. The church in the twentieth century is called to demonstrate the love of God in all its dealings with the world and its people. This way, even when the Scriptures are foreign, or obscure, or unavailable, God's people can be a universal language, ". . . known and read of all men" (II Corinthians 3:2, KJV). This is our highest calling as Christians. Here is the mature significance of the three little words taught in church school that take a lifetime to practice: "Love one another." In the heart of every individual is a primary hunger to love and to be loved. This can be fully satisfied only as a human being comes into the total belonging he experiences as he receives Jesus Christ as Saviour and Lord.

Also within the soul of man is a contrary tendency which rejoices in the unloving characteristics of others. It is easy to see the mote in our brother's eye and ignore the beam in our own! We often seek to lift ourselves by pulling others down. Such is our deceitful nature. Love, on the contrary, refuses to capitalize on the short-comings of others. Love implies caring—for better or for worse. Love is an active concern for the life and growth of that which we love. The very essence of love is to work for something and to help it grow. Love and labor are inseparable. You love what you work for, and you work hard for that which you love. Love rejoices in the accomplishment of what is honest and right. "[Love] is never glad about injustice, but rejoices whenever truth wins out" (I Corinthians 13:6).

On the negative side, love finds no satisfaction in that which is wrong. When you read that delinquency is at an all-time high, what does it do to you? When you hear about four boys bludgeoning a man to death, what do you feel inside? When you read of an innocent girl despoiled as she sleeps, or a child kidnapped and brutally slain for money, what is your reaction? When a thousand times a day, somewhere in this country, a gavel drops and a judge says, "Divorce granted!" does it bother you?

To the Christian, sin is sad. Love cannot find any satisfaction in evil. But God's truth, as it is revealed in the growth of those we love, those for whom we accept responsibility, is great joy for the concerned Christian. When we see a delinquent boy brought into the shelter of such a place as Christian Haven, or the Youth for Christ George Washington Home, and given a whole new life in Christ, it is cause for rejoicing. "Rejoice in the Lord always: and again I say, Rejoice" (Philippians 4:4, KJV). If we are called to spend hours with a couple on the verge of divorce, and they somehow sense God's love in our concern and attention, and their old love is reborn and enriched by a new love for God, then we can sing and shout for joy. "Delight thyself also in the Lord; and he shall give thee the desires of thine heart" (Psalms 37:4, KJV).

It is often very helpful amid the problems of our age to ask the question, "What would our Lord do in this situation? How would Jesus act with this person, or this couple?" Jesus Christ was loving; He was also uncompromising. At times His words were so piercing that the people wanted to kill Him.

It is true that He went about doing good, but His goodness was firm and His words stringent, and He called forth the best in the people He met. He gave offense to His disciples, to His relatives, to the scribes and Pharisees, for He was always obedient to a higher loyalty. On one occasion, Jesus said, "Think not that I am come to send peace on earth: I came not to send peace, but a sword" (Matthew 10:34, KJV).

Jesus was loving and kind, but His kind of love is firm. When it came to evil He was severe. God's love never rejoices in wrong, but rejoices in the right.

"If you love someone you will be loyal to him no matter what the cost" (I Corinthians 13:7). Love is protective. The word *beareth*, used in the *King James* translation, literally means to cover, shelter, or protect. Love is a retreat which shelters people from the storm. This pictorial word suggests placing a shield to shelter those underneath from danger. When a brother falls, what do you do? Do you lift him up, or cast him aside? Do you cover his faults, or whisper about them? Do you engage in character assassination, or do you try to

85

work directly with the one in trouble? Unkind talk hinders the work of God a thousand times over. Critical tongues close church doors to hundreds of people. Unnecessary talk breaks the hearts and health of many pastors. Someone has said, "A critical tongue is like Samson's foxes with firebrands on their tails going among the cornstalks of the Philistines."

A person says, "Did you hear the awful story about Mr. So-and-So? I was so sorry." He lies! He was glad, or else he would have kept it to himself. The gossip, the slanderer, is worse than the biggest thief in the world. The thief steals money, but the slanderer steals what money cannot buy—a man's reputation. A recognized weakness in someone else can make us feel superior as we talk about it, if we don't carefully ask for God's love in our reactions.

Our words can be more deadly than the poison of a snake. Paul says in Romans 3:13 (KJV). ". . . the poison of asps is under their lips." Common everyday griping and unnecessary criticism are poisons, in the Christian community and in our own souls.

Robert Burns, with great perception, writes about judging others:

<blockquote>
Who made the heart, 'tis He alone
    Decidedly can try us:
He knows each chord, its various tone,
    Each spring, its various bias:
Then at the balance let's be mute,
    We never can adjust it;
What's done we partly may compute,
    But know not what's resisted.
</blockquote>

Jesus said, "Judge not, that ye be not judged" (Matthew 7:1, KJV). When the scribes and Pharisees judged the woman caught in the act of adultery Jesus turned and said, "He that is without sin among you, let him first cast a stone at her" (John 8:7, KJV). Jesus judged them for judging the woman. Those who judge others will receive God's judgement. The Lord forgives and forgets, and so must we. Henry Ward Beecher put it this way: "God pardons like a mother, who kisses the offense into everlasting forgetfulness." Love bears all things, believes all things, hopes all things, and endures all things.

A great aid in helping us accept the failures of others is remembering that God has covered all of our sins—sins of long ago and sins of today, sins of the body, of the soul, of the spirit, sins of omission and commission. The Psalmist says: "As far as the east is from the west, so far hath he removed our transgressions from us" (Psalms 103:12, KJV). ". . . thou wilt cast all their sins into the depths of the sea" (Micah 7:19, KJV). "I have blotted out, as a thick cloud, thy transgressions" (Isaiah 44:22, KJV). ". . . thou hast cast all my sins behind thy back" (Isaiah 38:17, KJV). He has not only forgiven but forgotten: ". . . I will remember their sin no more" (Jeremiah 31:34, KJV). The Bible exhausts the possibility of language, in telling us how God completely forgives.

When Andrew Jackson was being questioned concerning church membership, the pastor asked, "General, there is one more question which I must ask you. Can you forgive all your enemies?" Andrew Jackson was silent as he recalled his stormy life of bitter fighting. Then he responded: "My political enemies I can freely forgive; but as for those who attacked me for serving my country, and those who slandered my wife . . . Doctor, I cannot forgive them!"

The pastor made it clear to Jackson that before he could become a member of that church and partake of the broken bread and the cup, his hatred and bitterness must be confessed and dealt with before God. Again there was an awkward silence, until Andrew Jackson affirmed that if God would help him, he would forgive his enemies.

There may be other occasions when we are called on to forgive our *friends*. Overreactions and under-reactions on the part of people very dear to us sometimes result in unbearable situations which can tie us up in knots and drain our effectiveness. Whether the friend or relative is actually at fault matters little. Our response to his behavior can be quiet annoyance, or it can be the violent explosion of a burst of temper, a crying spell, a sudden withdrawal, a jealous act, or an unkind retort.

A minister I know tells how he once was afraid to have any of the members of his congregation more spiritual than he was. One of the new members of this church was so in love with Christ that he couldn't stand her exhilarating influence in the congregation. First, he was upset after he had asked her to give the story of her conversion in the Sunday evening service—not because of her story, but because several people commented that it was the best service in months. It was hard for him to take because *he* had been preaching regularly at those other services!

Then he began to encounter such comments as, "Phyllis thinks it'd be a good idea," or "Phyllis suggested. . . ."

Then he found himself looking for ways to prove that Phyllis's ideas wouldn't work. He figured out ways to prove that she needed him. He looked for opportunities to show her that she really didn't know as much about spiritual things as she thought she did.

It was the new Christian in this case who asked for a confrontation. She said, bearing the conflict in love, "You are my pastor, and I need you. We seem to be fighting each other. We shouldn't do that. We're on the same side." She even asked his forgiveness for being hard to live with.

For two and a half hours they talked. The pastor found it humbling, even embarrassing. But this new convert, this woman, helped him find himself. He was forgiven in a genuine outreach of love, and he in turn could ask forgiveness in a pouring out of the competitive spirit and jealousy which had grounded his ministry.

What a release! Within a few months his whole congregation felt the new freedom. His sermons improved. Phyllis's love that bore his unjust combat enabled him finally to forgive and to profit from the bad feelings he had harbored.

An unforgiving spirit blocks the forgiveness of God. Booker T. Washington said, "I will not permit any man to narrow and degrade my soul by making me hate him." A delicious sense of peace comes to the one who learns how to forgive. Love bears all that is placed upon its shoulders and covers all that is placed beneath its wings. "He who cannot forgive others breaks the bridge over which he must pass himself," wrote George Herbert.

When you are tempted to gripe and complain about someone, remember the Scripture: ". . . be ye kind one

to another, tenderhearted, forgiving one another, even
as God for Christ's sake hath forgiven you" (Ephesians
4:32, KJV). What a measure of forgiving spirit!

You will always believe in him . . . [I Corinthians
13:7].

Love takes the kindest view possible of people and
circumstances. Love searches for what is good and gives
the benefit when in doubt.

A helpful prayer experiment began some years ago in
Pittsburgh. A group of Christian businessmen saw very
practical results of this expression of love—this believing
in people—as they got under the burden with some men
who were unemployed. As they became willing to spend
time with these men who were out of a job, they began
to love them, to pray for them and with them.

One of the most interesting results of this communication of love through prayer lay in the response of the
two hundred men who found employment during a
nineteen-month period. It became apparent that most of
them were finding their own jobs as this fellowship of
love gave them increased confidence in themselves and
renewed faith in God's personal concern for them. As a
result of Christ's men believing in them, they were able
to believe in themselves and move ahead.

One man said he left the first meeting and began
to pray regularly that he would find a job. Sometime
later, while preparing for his daily period of prayer,
he stopped a moment and said to himself, "Mel, you've
just been praying for work. Perhaps it's time to pray
that the Lord will strengthen your faith." The next day
the phone rang, and a man who had interviewed him

90

some weeks before asked if he were still looking for employment. The very next day he went to work. Love has faith. Love trusts. Love believes in—inspires, lifts up.

The results in opening new doors to employment, in contacting people who were hiring around the city, were not coincidences. The men who were communicating God's love had no magic formula. But the results they could see were far beyond their limited human means.

. . . always expect the best of him . . . [I Corinthians 13:7].

Hope and great expectations are the antidotes for despair and gloom. For the most part I have been an optimist. People who are born with the kind of temperament that finds it easy to be sunny seem to have a bit of a head start in life. Someone has defined optimism as a cheerful frame of mind that enables a teakettle to sing, though in hot water up to its nose. I am an optimist chiefly because I recognize that God is sovereign and His triumph is sure.

The Psalmist sang, "I will bless the Lord at all times: his praise shall continually be in my mouth" (Psalm 34:1, KJV). David did not live a sheltered life. Saul hated him; Absalom rebelled against him; his baby died. Still his pattern of life was one of trust and hope. Love hopes in every conceivable experience. Love is optimistic, not pessimistic. This is not a blind optimism, but a confidence based on God and His word. To the sinful, the Saviour said, ". . . be of good cheer; thy sins be forgiven thee" (Matthew 9:2, KJV). This is not empty sentimental talk; here is the most revolutionary statement a man can hear. There is hope for all who will turn to the Saviour for forgiveness. Nothing in all the world can cheer a person like the forgiveness of sin. "Blessed is he whose transgression is forgiven, whose sin is covered" (Psalms 32:1, KJV).

To the fearful our Lord speaks: "Be of good cheer; it is I; be not afraid" (Matthew 14:27, KJV). These words were uttered to frightened men. Love is God's cure for fear. It shows up all the time—in our business procedures, our children's grades at school, our dating and marital practices, our attitude towards new assignments and new people. "There is no fear in love; but perfect love casteth out fear: because fear hath torment. He that feareth is not made perfect in love" (I John 4:18, KJV). Love opens up the heart, the mind, the hand, the purse. Fear clamps down on everything.

Some of our Christian efforts in the ghetto keep turning up evidence of what happens when young people come in contact with love that expects the best of them. Some who have floundered through school with D's, demerits and detentions, not caring a fig for the marks they were making, have literally come alive when they met Christ. For the first time they have found a reason for trying, a purpose in doing their best, and we have seen boys and girls straighten up and graduate from high school, instead of dropping out. One fellow said, "Before I met the Lord I had a *D* average going into my senior year. The school told me, 'You can quit.' But when I really heard how much Christ loved me, I prayed, 'Christ, if you're real, you better do something in my life, 'cause I need it.' I came back to school and made the honor roll at the end of my senior year, passed my college boards and they let me in college."

The terrified disciples, seeing a figure upon the waters, said, "It is a spirit" (Matthew 14:26, KJV), and cried out for fear. These experienced fishermen had passed through many storms, but they are not prepared for a spirit walking on the water. The unexplained experiences of life are always the most frightening, but God's presence gives abundant cause for hope. Love expects the best in everything.

. . . and always stand your ground in defending him [I Corinthians 13:7].

Love has an enduring quality. Through good times and bad times, glad days and sad days, through doubt and darkness, love is persistent. It has the power to take it even when it lacks the power to believe or hope. Love holds its ground. The Christian experience is not a picnic. Samuel Rutherford said, "You will not be carried to heaven lying at ease upon a feather bed."

Jeanie is a young, suburban high-school girl who met Christ at a summer camp. This new love in her life has given her the ability to look clearly at herself and her family. Her acceptance of Jesus Christ as her personal Saviour did not remove the hard things in her life, but it has given her fresh insights about them. "My greatest fault," she says, "was cutting down kids. I never even gave it a thought before. Now I can see how cruel this is. When I start to rip someone apart now, I suddenly realize how mean and selfish I am."

She also has a new attitude toward her father, a salesman caught in the liquor routine. She used to avoid him and resent him as a mean man. One of the first evidences of God's new love flowing into Jeanie's life came almost immediately after she said "yes" to Christ. "I wanted to get home right away," she recalls. "I was afraid my mom was so lonely. I had always taken her for granted, and, all of a sudden, I began to see that my dad was really sick, not mean."

Jesus said, "In the world ye shall have tribulation; but be of good cheer; I have overcome the world" (John 16:33, KJV). Here is sufficient reason for optimism. Trials? Yes, but these tribulations are merely opportunities to display God's power and love. This enduring love is Godlike. "Love bears all things, believes all things, hopes all things, endures all things" (I Corinthians 13:7, RSV).

Some time ago the area where we were living experienced a terrible forest fire. The marks of the conflagration were thoroughly depressing. As I walked through the forest I doubted if anything had survived the inferno. All looked hopelessly dead. Blackness prevailed. Six months later I went again and witnessed a miracle. Nature, with a lush mantle of green, had covered the darkness, overflowed the wounds, and hidden the scars. I walked in the midst of nature's profusion of goodness and prayed:

> *Dear Lord, help me to live like this. Let Thy love flow through me to cover the shortcomings, the wounds, the angry scars which make all of us difficult to love. Give me an understanding heart. Amen.*

VIII. LOVE NEVER FAILS

VIII. LOVE NEVER FAILS

VIII

Love Never Fails

We live in an exciting age of progress. Man has split and fused the atom, placing tremendous energy at his disposal. He has attained speeds of travel unknown to any other generation.

In 1927 Charles Lindbergh crossed the Atlantic, flying at a speed of about 100 miles an hour and an altitude of 5,000 feet. Today the YF-12A flies 2,062 miles an hour at 80,000 feet. Soon the supersonic jet will be in operation. San Francisco will be only two hours from New York; and Paris will be just under three hours from New York! Serious study is being given to hypersonic transport, which deals with speeds up to 7,000 miles per hour.

United Airlines estimates that by 1990 rockets will be sufficiently developed for commercial transportation, so that we can blast off from New York and make a soft landing in Manila—17,000 miles away—in about 45 minutes. Stupendous, isn't it? We have seen more material changes in the last one hundred years than in all recorded history, and yet, our big concern is still how to relate to each other successfully.

Lillian Smith, late author and outspoken champion of racial equality, talked about how the twentieth century is becoming the age of human relations. Suddenly, we are only a few hours from everyone on earth, and men can collaborate as they never have before on problem solving. At the same time, modern technology gives us new instruments and insights with which we can examine and understand ourselves. "It has crept upon us so quietly," she wrote in *The Journey*. "We have hardly noticed. But it is one of the significant events of the twentieth century: these groups of men and women, finding their tongues, sloughing off the old mutism and doing it just as science gives them the means of world-wide communication. Not arguing, not debating, not defending and entrenching their past mistakes. Not on trial. Simply saying, 'It was this way with me.'"

Too often we Christians in our churches have not provided opportunity for people to express how it is with them. The church is a classic example of a situation where we can get together with four hundred or four thousand people on a Sunday morning and not really know any of them. We can participate in a truly significant experience of encountering God, without ever really encountering the person sitting with us in the pew.

A minister in the pastoral care department of one of Chicago's newest hospitals feels the Christian church today has a tremendous potential which has scarcely been tapped. "Our churches are worship-centered," says Pastor Larry Holst, "and project-centered, but not person-centered. The individual Christian often does not experience the kind of community where he can be himself, or where he can confront his fellow human beings in all of their weaknesses and strengths. He needs

98

the opportunity for openness and confrontation—a group experience where he can be honest with others and with himself, where he can discuss his doubts, his fears, his anguishes, his griefs, his frustrations. Christian fellowship is coming to see our humanity and all that it means— the splendor and the grandeur of man created in the image of God, as well as his misery, the potential of man in Christ, as well as his sinfulness. If we could get our congregations to be sensitive to the inter-personal feelings and relationships that are so crucial to people, I think we could turn many of our 'sleeping giants' into powerhouses of God's healing love."

The thing that most often causes people to collapse is the lack or loss of meaning in life. People find meaning in many different things: appearance, youthfulness, sexuality, vocation, children, education, pleasure, and many others. But when these meanings are threatened, the person collapses. Life does not allow us the luxury of indulging ourselves in an impoverished past. People need to be encouraged to take the risk of being hurt again, once they have been stepped on or bruised. This can only occur on a lasting level when they can come into contact with the love of God, through His loving people in this world.

The ancient sophists used to say, "Nothing will last." However, in direct contrast, Paul the Apostle tells us that love is sure and lasting: love ". . . never faileth . . ." (I Corinthians 13:8, KJV).

To meet this need for an experience of the love that does not fail, some churches are starting small groups where individuals can know each other, where they can begin to impart the love of Christ to each other. Love is the dynamic that is so revolutionary in life. We have always had it, and we have always proclaimed it, but maybe we should ask ourselves if we are experiencing it in as many interpersonal ways as we can within our own congregations. Perhaps we should ask, "Does a person who comes into our church sense a real acceptance in love, or does he only hear about it?"

The word *fail* has two technical meanings. The classical Greek presents the picture of a bad actor being hissed off the stage. Of course, love is not like this, as it lives on even on the stage of eternity. Love is never hissed off the stage. The other picture is of a fading flower with falling petals. Love never withers, fades, nor falls away. Love never loses its place.

Paul spoke about unusual spiritual gifts—the gift of prophecy, the ability to speak, and knowledge. These God-given gifts, he said, would terminate, but love lasts. Love is the most enduring virtue in this world. When we wish to speak of lasting things, we allude to the everlasting hills and the unchanging heavens, but even these symbols of permanency undergo change. All about us we see the elements wasting under the powers of corruption. Giant trees, once monarchs of the forest, are now bent and broken with age. All nature groans under this process of death. The Bible says, ". . . all the hills shall melt" (Amos 9:13, KJV). As to the unchanging heavens, we read, ". . . as a vesture shalt thou fold them up, and they shall be changed" (Hebrews 1:12, KJV). Let us remember that ". . . the things which are seen are temporal; but the things which are not seen are eternal" (II Corinthians 4:18, KJV).

Where are the lavish, exotic Hanging Gardens of

Babylon? They are all gone. Where are the majestic temples of Greece? For the most part, they are broken memories of the Golden Age. The great empires of yesterday have been led to the tomb by the hand of time.

Death uproots and pulls down all creation. Every field has a grave, every city a cemetery. This ugly invader not only turns creation's beauty to ashes but brings the creature to dust. Death darkens the eyes of those we love; it eventually shakes our own limbs, and shuts the door on this life. Mortality reigns in our bodies. Death starts at birth. The mills of time grind slowly—but never forget, they grind fine.

In complete contrast, love never dies. Though everything else is mortal, love is immortal. When all else fails, love never fails. An accurate translation could be, "Love never falls down on the job." It not only never fails, it never ends. Though tongues cease and knowledge vanishes, love lasts.

Jealousy over spiritual gifts had gripped the Corinthian Christians. This is probably why Paul stressed that the greatest gift is love for each member of the body of Christ, no matter how unimportant he might seem. Love was for the Corinthians; love is for you, too.

The history of the world has been one of greed, selfishness and war, rather than love. Emerson, in "Man, The Reformer," said, "Love would put a new face on this weary old world in which we dwell as pagans and enemies too long, and it would warm the heart to see how fast the vain diplomacy of statesmen, the impotence of armies, and navies, and lines of defence, would be superseded by this unarmed child. Love will creep where it cannot go, will accomplish that by imperceptible

101

methods,—being its own lever, fulcrum, and power,—which force could never achieve."

Love is powerful beyond our comprehension. Jesus Christ demonstrated this power in life and in death. The cross continues to display God's love and His power of forgiveness.

Jesus Christ is the fulfillment of every characteristic listed by the Apostle. It would be absolutely right to say that Jesus Christ never fails.

We have seen how most things in life fail. Money fails. Fame fails. The world, writes John, passes away. Sometimes business fails. Governments fail. Friends often let us down. Health fails. In fact, everything fails except that which is centered in Christ. ". . . Christ in you, the hope of Glory . . ." (Colossians 1:27, KJV).

The Apostle Peter failed our Lord. He followed afar off and denied Christ on three successive opportunities. He said he would die with Him, but he openly denied his Lord.

Thomas failed. When the disciples spoke of the resurrection he doubted and said, "Except I shall see in his hands the prints of the nails, and put my finger into the print of the nails, and thrust my hand into his side, I will not believe" (John 20:25, KJV).

The disciples failed. After His Gethsemane experience, ". . . the disciples forsook him, and fled" (Matthew 26:56, KJV). They let Him down.

It is comforting to realize that the failure of the disciples did not alter Christ's love for them. Eventually Peter wept bitterly at his coolness. Thomas cried out, "My Lord and My God" (John 21:28, KJV). The disciples came back for cleansing and renewal. We in the twentieth century fail Him too, but He cannot fail us, for He is God. His love is eternal. The greatest adventure in life is to experience the love of God in Jesus Christ and to transmit it to others, for then all that we do will be eternal. The mission He has given us is: "This I command you, to love one another" (John 15:17, RSV).

Millions of people viewed Michelangelo's famous "Pieta," on exhibit at the New York World's Fair. It is a sculpture of the crucified Christ in the arms of Mary. It has been called marble in rhythm. Some day this masterpiece will crumble and the name of its creator will be forgotten, but a deed which is performed in love will last forever. To be motivated by God's love is to live with eternity in view in every situation we face during a day. The great paintings of the masters will all pass into oblivion, but our acts of love will abide.

Recently I visited the 102-story, 1472-foot Empire State Building, the tallest man-made structure on earth. It is a fantastic architectural feat, but some day the tons of concrete will be broken and the designer remembered no more; yet a cup of cold water, which you are willing to give in love, will break upon the shores of eternity. Love lasts. Love never fails. Let us pray daily for this gift of love, this experience of containing the Someone who *is* love. Let us dare to ask boldly that we may find the greatest marvel of all time, the greatest realization of ourselves. Let us seek humbly the clarity, the openness in our lives that enables our human associates to feel loved by us, and to say in wonder, "God is there!"

Heavenly Father, I thank Thee for the permanency of love. "So we do not look at what we can see down here, the troubles

103

all around us, but we look forward to the joys of heaven which we have not yet seen. The troubles will soon go away, but the joys to come will last forever" (II Corinthians 4:18). *Amen.*

IX. THE SOURCE OF LOVE

IX
The Source of Love

The source of love is God. That is where love comes from, for God is love. There are endless stories of the changes that occur in people's lives when they experience the happiness, the glory of God's love. Love is really the aliveness, the responsiveness of God's Holy Spirit in us. We cannot have one without the other. What life is to the physical body, the Holy Spirit is to our spirit. A great many people make the mistake of struggling to get the fruits of the Spirit without ever opening themselves up to the Spirit himself. This kind of effort is in vain. The secret of the fullness of love is the fullness of the Spirit of God. Paul the Apostle tells us plainly, ". . . the love of God is shed abroad in our hearts by the Holy Ghost which is given unto us" (Romans 5:5, KJV).

A group of former narcotic addicts is saying the same thing in the twentieth century. On heroin from four to sixteen years, they came to Jesus Christ because they had tried everything else and had found no way out. John Giminez of New York City describes the experience of delivery from drugs through the gift of the Holy Spirit:

"God brings His Holy Spirit into messed up humans. That bursting forth of the Spirit within us is so peaceful and beautiful and sweet! We struggled so hard for so long to keep our bodies satisfied, and suddenly here was this wonderful Holy Spirit satisfying both our flesh and our spirit. . . . When we come home to God we get loved like we never have been loved before by anyone. We can walk with our heads up, and smiles on our faces. . . . Since we discovered that God really loves us, and it doesn't matter anymore all the terrible things we have done, then we got to try to help other people make the same discovery we made. . . . We know what it feels like to be lost. But we know now what it feels like to come home. We can see all the wonderful possibilities in a person. In a girls' prison, for instance, we can tell them, 'God loves and cares for you.' We can see ahead what God has for them when they come to Him. They can be fit mothers and loving wives. We know that God can do this for them because He has done so much for us."

Let us go back to the very beginning. The very first step is to receive Jesus Christ as Saviour. He is God's gift of love to you. Without this salvation experience you will find everything else impossible. Jesus said, "Verily, verily, I say unto thee, Except a man be born again, he cannot see the kingdom of God" (John 3:3, KJV).

The first step is to know that you need help. So many people want to be right in their own eyes, respectable in others' eyes, rather than truly well. You need first of all to face the fact that you are not whole; you are not well; you are not capable of making it by yourself. Sin is missing the mark of God's standard, and we all fit that description. It is willful disobedience, or lack of obedience to God's written Word and to the living Word,

108

Jesus Christ. The Scriptures remind us, "All the world [is] guilty before God" (Romans 3:19, KJV). The second step is to recognize Jesus Christ as God's Saviour for human beings.

When you understand that Christ is God's remedy, that God—in His love—made this whole magnificent arrangement so you can be complete as a person, then you will want to ask His forgiveness for your sin. "But as many as received him, to them gave he power to become the sons of God, even to them that believe on his name" (John 1:12, KJV). We believe God, receive His answer to our dilemma, and we become children of God! That's what He said—*children of God!* To know anything about the love of God, one must truly know God. Love is not a law or a code, but a Person. This is one of the most remarkable things about the Christian faith. God knew we could not know love until we had felt it, experienced it. So He expressed His love in a human form—Jesus Christ—so that we human beings could grasp the patience, the kindness, the humbleness, the confidence, the optimism, the joy that is contained in His perfect love. The important question, then, is this: Do you know Jesus Christ? Have you invited Him into your life to be the power that will make you a brand new person—a child of God?

The Scripture plainly teaches that when you do this, you actually become the dwelling place of the Holy Spirit. This is a staggering truth! Think of it—God the Holy Spirit, residing in every one who believes!

Paul put it this way, "Know ye not that ye are the temple of God, and that the Spirit of God dwelleth in you?" (I Corinthians 3:16, KJV).

In times past God was in the tabernacle and then in the temple. Where is He now? The Bible says, ". . . Christ in you, the hope of glory" (Colossians 1:27, KJV). Whether you are eight years old or eighty, the moment you receive Christ, the Holy Spirit comes to live in your body. The word *dwell* used in the verse above has a beautiful depth of meaning. It means to settle down to stay, permanently, as we do in our own homes. The Holy Spirit is a personal, permanent Guest. The Holy Spirit is God in us *all the time*.

But He is not there just to be taken for granted. The Holy Spirit may be grieved because of our carelessness. Paul warns, ". . . grieve not the Holy Spirit of God, whereby ye are sealed unto the day of redemption" (Ephesians 4:30, KJV). The word *grieve* means to cause sorrow. Dr. G. Campbell Morgan asked, "How would you like to be compelled to live with somebody who was everlastingly grieving your heart by his conduct?" How terrible we feel when we hurt someone we love! We would do *anything* to make amends for the disappointment, the heartbreak we have caused the beloved. Let us not grieve or quench the indwelling Holy Spirit. He is the source of love in us. May we rather ". . . be filled with the Spirit" (Ephesians 5:18).

"But how can I do this?" you ask. The fullness of the Spirit is dependent upon your yieldedness. When you want God's will in your life, you will think, talk, walk, and live in this desire. This is the happy relationship of love. " It is not *my* love," you will say, but *His* love; not *my* ability but *His* ability in me."

Under normal and natural human conditions, you are not inclined to sacrifice and suffer for others, but when you are dominated by the Holy Spirit, love and sacrifice spring spontaneously to your mind and heart. You begin to see people in new ways. You recognize selfishness in yourself, and needs in others, that you never saw before. The natural man loves the praise of the people all around him, while the Spirit-filled person yearns for the praise of God. To know real fullness of love you must allow a change in your heart, a change of focus from self to Christ. This change comes from wanting God's Holy Spirit in the "driver's seat" of your life, instead of yourself. It results in God's love working *in* you, and out to others *through* you.

Just as you accepted new life by faith in Christ, you are to accept and trust the fullness of the Spirit which He promises us, by faith. Paul, writing to the Galatians, states ". . . receive the promise of the Spirit through faith" (Galatians 3:14, KJV). "Through faith" places this gift within reach of each believer. The youngest Christian can understand this and know this fullness of love. Do not look at yourself and your shortcomings and get depressed and bogged down. The disciples could see the hopelessness of living a life of love in their own strength. They knew it was impossible, and so do you. But the great good news is just this: God knew it too! Look at Jesus Christ and His faithfulness. God's perfect character stands behind His promises. His perfect love will fill us if we let it. Don't struggle—*believe!*

Paul says, ". . . the fruit of the Spirit is love . . ." (Galatians 5:22, KJV). Don't get worried and hasty now. Fruit comes slowly. It takes a seed, a flower, pollenization, warm sunshine, cold rains, and contrary winds to produce the finished fruit. That's true in life, too.

111

Our lives are made up of sunshine and rain, laughter and tears, black skies, harsh winds, pruning shears. There are valleys as well as mountain peaks. All of these work to produce this precious fruit called love. Are you yielding to the Holy Spirit? Do you know what it is to demonstrate love? All other gifts you may possess are less important than this fruit of the Holy Spirit. Let this love that comes from God be plentiful in our lives. The nine-fold fruit of the Spirit is the reproduction of the life and love of Jesus Christ in us.

A little girl was busily playing with her dolls when suddenly she left them and climbed upon her mother's lap to hug and kiss her affectionately. The surprised mother asked, "Why did you leave your dolls and come to Mother?" The simple, childish answer was, "Mother, I love my dolls, but my dollies never love me back." How important it is to be loved! God has given each one of us a free will. We are not mechanical robots. How wonderful it is to tell the Lord that we love Him earnestly. Even with all our faults we can, so to speak, climb on His lap and love Him. There is nothing that gives Him greater joy than our childlike response to His magnificent love.

D. L. Moody relates this incident in his life: "One day in New York, oh, what a day, I cannot describe it, I seldom refer to it, it is almost too sacred an experience to name; I can only say God revealed Himself to me. I had such an experience of His love that I had to ask Him to stay His hand. I went to preaching again; the sermons were no different, I did not present any new truth, yet hundreds were converted, and I would not be placed back where I was before that blessed experience if you would give me all Glasgow." Moody had had such a great hunger and thirst after God's fullness that he had searched—yes, even pleaded—for God to fill him. Do you really hunger and thirst for this love?

In our world, love shows itself by action. Our Lord said, "Ye shall know them by their fruits" (Matthew 7:16, KJV). This means that our service, our behavior, will be a test of our love for Christ. But Jesus went even further when He said, "Not every one that saith unto me, Lord, Lord, shall enter into the kingdom of heaven; but he that doeth the will of my Father which is in heaven" (Matthew 7:21, KJV). And again, He said, "If ye love me, keep my commandments" (John 14:15, KJV). "He that hath my commandments, and keepeth them, he it is that loveth me" (v. 21). "By this shall all men know that you are my disciples, if you have love one to another" (John 13:35, KJV). It is all very plain. We can hardly mistake His meaning.

What is the proof of love? Love itself. One day the risen Christ talked with Simon Peter, the denier, with this question, "Simon, son of Jonas, lovest thou me more than these?" (John 21:15, KJV). When Peter answered, "Yea, Lord," the Saviour said, "Feed my lambs." Jesus repeated the same question and Peter gave the same answer. Then the Saviour said, "Feed my sheep (v. 16)." Jesus questioned Simon the third time (as many times as Peter had denied Christ). At this continued pressing, the Scripture tells us, "Peter was grieved. . . . And he said unto him, Lord, thou knowest all things; thou knowest that I love thee. Jesus saith unto him, Feed my sheep" (v. 19). Jesus was emphasizing the necessary relationship between *loving* and *feeding* the sheep.

Real love always serves. It lasts! Love is not content to sit and do nothing. Love is active. It has to express itself in giving, in serving, in being. The proof of our love comes in our ability and our willingness to help other people. The high-school girl who used to "cut down kids," now sees the selfishness in this practice. She has a God-given desire to understand the shortcomings of her friends now—as well as her own. She wants to pray for them and help them understand themselves. The woman who had heard rumors about the two women who lived alone found that the love of God overcame her concern, her fear, so that she was able to share abroad the love of Christ in a home that literally had fallen apart without love.

One woman who was at her wit's end tells of this experience. During a long winter, sickness and accident had struck just about everyone in her family. Mumps, measles, a broken nose, a broken leg, and four new teeth for the baby made pressures and demands accumulate till she fell on her knees to protest in desperation, "Oh, Lord! I have so much to do!" To her astonishment, what came out was quite different. The words she heard herself cry out instead were these: "Oh, Lord! I have so much to *love!*"

What a difference there is in life when we can transpose those two little words. How many ways we can find to express that love: planting hope where there is no hope; listening to the cry of a rebellious teen-ager; soothing the pain of a hospital patient; giving cool water to a dying enemy on the battlefield; visiting the shut-in; helping the widow and taking in the orphan; and ministering to the man in prison. We can leave a pot of soup

114

for the woman just out of the hospital; collect money to help an elderly couple whose home was burned; share a flower with someone who is sad; help a blind person to a chair in the station; cuddle a lost child; share breakfast with a man on skid row. We can counsel high-school people at a summer camp, discuss our own experience of God's love with the neighbor child who comes to chat; talk with the woman next door; invite the man in our office to go fishing with us.

There are countless millions of ways in which the Holy Spirit will ask us to love, as we yield our seconds, our minutes, our days to Him—as we hold up our friendships, our difficult relationships, our families, our encounters with strangers to Him. Love cannot sit still and do nothing. It will eagerly look for the day when the King of love will come in person, but it has to be demonstrating His love to love-starved people while it looks. Love is action, and the proof of your love for Jesus Christ will be found in your service to others. The nurse's aide in the hospital who gently washes the hands, the legs, the feet of the man dying of cancer, is getting very close to the example of Christ as He washed His disciples' feet. ". . . as ye have done it unto one of . . . these . . . ye have done it unto me" (Matthew 25:40, KJV), He said.

I do not mean by all of this that we must always be on the go. Surely we must worship before we work; meditation must precede ministering, being tuned in to the Spirit precedes being tuned in to others. There must always be that retirement in which our soul is prepared for action. We have become very much a meeting-oriented people. We go, go, go. Arnold J. Toynbee, in

115

his *Study of History*, writes of history being composed of "a moment of withdrawal." To serve without preparation is to thoroughly exhaust oneself. When the crowds sought to make Jesus King, He departed into His mountain retreat. Before He began His public ministry, He spent forty days in the wilderness. Our Lord practiced moments of withdrawal. The early Christians gave themselves to prayer and communion which in turn resulted in service. How much more do we in this jet age need to worship Christ before we can work for Christ? ". . . they that wait upon the Lord shall renew their strength; they shall mount up with wings as eagles; they shall run, and not be weary; and they shall walk, and not faint" (Isaiah 40:31, KJV).

Mary chose to sit at the feet of Jesus while Martha served. When you are yielded to the Holy Spirit, your worship and work will be blended together. Service is the fruit of worship. The fullness of love comes only through the fullness of the Holy Spirit.

> *Heavenly Father, more than anything in life we want the fullness of the Holy Spirit. In childlike faith we yield ourselves completely. May the Holy Spirit love this world through us in each activity this day. Amen.*

X. LOVE LOST AND FOUND

X

Love Lost and Found

Edmund Burke, in one of his speeches on English politics, mentions the decline of character in a civil statesman. He says, "The instances are exceedingly rare of men immediately passing over a clear marked line from virtue into declared vice and corruption. There are middle tints and shades between the two extremes; there is something uncertain on the confines of the two empires which they must pass through, and which renders the change easy and imperceptible."

This is often true in the spiritual realm. Samson exposed himself to evil until a moral paralysis made him oblivious to God's absence, "And he wist not that the Lord was departed from him" (Judges 16:20, KJV). The early days of King Saul were like a magnificent sunrise; only gradually did the clouds appear until blackness triumphed.

The Ephesian believers were rebuked because they left their first love. These Christians were industrious, God-fearing, truth-abiding people, but they lost their original drive and devotion to the Lord. "I have somewhat against Thee, because thou hast left thy first love" (Revelation 2:4). History reveals that this process continued until the Ephesian church died.

What is that first love? It is that exciting flood of response that we experienced when the Spirit of God plainly assured us, "As far as the east is from the west, so far hath he removed our transgressions from us" (Psalms 103:12, KJV). First love is felt with the total trust and the warm affection of the newborn soul. First love looks at the grand possibilities, not the weight of the problems. Each river is a stirring challenge to cross; each mountain an adventure to climb. Stumbling stones become stepping stones. Every obstacle is a fresh way to prove the omnipotence of God. First love is warm, kind, radiant, and real. With wide-open arms, first love welcomes the world to its heart. It wears working trousers in the market place; it gets in gear with real people who have deep needs. This love is clean, expectant, strong, involved and victorious.

The Apostle Paul knew this kind of love firsthand. Besides possessing a brilliant mind, he was endowed with a loving heart. His soul was a furnace of concern for his generation. Writing to the people of Rome, he said, "I am debtor both to the Greeks and to the Barbarians; both to the wise, and to the unwise" (Romans 1:14, KJV). To the Thessalonian church he wrote, "For ye remember, brethren, our labour and travail: for labouring night and day, because we would not be chargeable unto any of you, we preached unto you the gospel of God" (I Thessalonians 2:9, KJV). The word *travail* indicates a deep concern, a struggle, even pain. Day and night Paul labored so that he would not be indebted to his generation. I can hear him say, "I have a debt, I have an obligation, I must share the gospel." To experience

120

real salvation is to love people. Personal salvation and loving people are synonomous. To remain self-centered and silent in the light of redemption is to become some sort of monster.

One of the faces of love is a willingness to be involved in another person's pain. And you might as well know right away that this will mean that you are going to suffer, too, along with the one who is troubled. Loving is not easy and not free of hurt. We human beings are constructed in a very complex way. It is our natural tendency to avoid pain. We do not like to feel uncomfortable. We are masters at building protective devices into our lives. When we experience rejection at the hand of another person, we almost unconsciously begin to figure how we can avoid that kind of hurt again. When someone screams at us, or spits out some spiteful comment, our natural reaction is to protect our own self-image by talking back, or screaming louder. We are exceedingly clever at defending ourselves from hurt, from pain, from discomfort. Only as we keep receiving the love of God into the big, demanding hole of self, are we prepared to take on the pain, the travail that Paul talked about.

The intensity of Paul's involvement is seen in depth in Romans 9:2: ". . . I have great heaviness and continual sorrow in my heart. For I could wish that myself were accursed from Christ for my brethren, my kinsmen according to the flesh" (KJV). This is redemptive love. In plain talk, Paul is saying, "I am prepared to go to hell, if by so doing my friends and countrymen will share in the gospel." Isn't this staggering? This kind of love is difficult to comprehend. This same spirit was shared by Moses when he interceded for Israel. Moses prayed, "Oh this people have sinned a great sin, and have made them gods of gold. Yet now, if thou wilt forgive their sin; and if not, blot me, I pray thee, out of thy book which thou hast written" (Exodus 32:31-32, KJV). Oh, what love! What identification! Both Moses and Paul were motivated by supernatural love.

The Ephesian believers were hard-working, patient, preserving and thoroughly orthodox. The Apostle John commended them for many virtues. The Christ of the candlesticks is not blind to the beauties of His people. He loves us and gave His life for us. He desires to see our light burning brightly. However, in spite of the outstanding virtues of the Ephesian church, the Lord of the lampstands could tell when their love declined into a noisy Pharisaic busyness. With the pain of a neglected love, He calls, "I have somewhat against Thee . . ." (Revelation 2:4, KJV).

How is this love lost? First love is lost because of sin, according to Matthew 24:12: ". . . because iniquity shall abound, the love of many shall wax cold" (KJV). Centuries ago Isaiah said, ". . . your iniquities have separated between you and your God, and your sins have hid his face from you, that he will not hear" (Isaiah 59:2, KJV). Sin dulls first love. It is a wall of separation that builds up between man and God. Sin darkens the light of our life. It blurs our understanding of the mind of God. Sin drains our spiritual power.

I heard a story once of an American eagle that was observed soaring magnificently into the sky. Shortly it faltered, stopped, and plunged toward the earth, dead. When the eagle was examined, it was discovered that a small weasel had dug its claws into the abdomen of the bird, risen with the eagle into the sky, and drained the life-blood while the eagle tried to escape. Sin is like that. It robs us of power and life itself. If we take a friendly attitude toward evil, then the Lord may take harsh measures with us. Sin is an obstacle to first love. It appears in two main forms—open rebellion against God, and a neglect of obedience to the revealed will of God. One of the prevailing problems of the church today is the obsession to be accepted. We get too concerned about what people will think. Sophistication has all but smothered first love. The church is on an intellectual binge to the point of cancelling the effect of the cross. Sometimes we Christians are so tactful that we don't make contact at all. Paul the Apostle, with all of his brilliance, would not permit the wisdom of this world to cancel out the power of the gospel. "For the preaching of the cross is to them that perish foolishness; but unto us which are saved it is the power of God" (I Corinthians 1:18, KJV). All sin has a chilling effect on first love.

Another way we lose the love we first knew is by trying to enshrine it and preserve it, by failing to let it bubble up through all of our living experience. Perhaps the clearest way to describe this failing of love is to draw a parallel within the stage of human marriage. The first tremendously overwhelming stage is what we have come to call *falling in love*. It is so urgent, so total that we stand alone with our beloved as though there were no one else in all the world. We want to retain the flame, the intensity, the one-and-only feeling forever. So we marry—for keeps—but soon we begin to discover that the world is still with us after all. We are not two people alone in a miraculous vacuum of love. We are a bit surprised to learn that we still have parents and in-laws, brothers and sisters, business associates and neighbors, old friends and strangers at the door. And somehow we have to begin to make room for all of these "presences" in our new life together. It takes time. It takes arguments and tears. These persons make demands on our marriage relationship which we don't particularly want. But we either learn how to keep our love warm and alive, while accomodating other people, or we get drawn into the complex process, and pulled away from our loved one. People, appointments, work, and a thousand other things, begin to pry us apart, and before we know it, the separation is almost unbridgeable. We look back across the gulf and say, "She's not the same person I married. We have so little in common. We really aren't compatible at all."

Is it possible that we as Christians fail in this same way as we begin to get involved in *service?* As we begin to stand back and look at this revolutionary love that has demanded total commitment of us, what do we see? Do we get so preoccupied with going to meetings, sounding well when we pray out loud, working on church committees or organizations, meeting the local standards of church behavior, watching our own piety become noticeable to others, that we lose sight of—don't have time for—the great Lover who first won us?

What happens as *you* begin to integrate this new love into your home life, your marriage, your office routine, your shop conversations, your school work? Do you stay in tune with the wondrous love that won you, and let the Holy Spirit show you how to share this freshness with others? Or do you hug it to yourself for fear of losing it, for fear of failing? Do you get so busy with your chores, your deadlines, your concern with what others think, that you lose touch with the Holy Spirit and wonder if the experience was ever real in the first place?

The big, and very practical, question is, "How is first love restored?" The Lord is always found exactly where we left Him. He calls out, "Remember . . . from whence thou art fallen" (Revelation 2:5, KJV). Remember when you enjoyed the presence of God in everyday living? Can you recall the moments of satisfying communion in prayer? Remember when the hymns of the church sang often in your mind through the day's work? Remember when you wept, unashamedly and joyously, out of gratitude to God for His goodness upon your life? Remember when you sought out loved ones and friends to tell them what Jesus was doing for you? "Remember, from whence thou art fallen."

Holy memories should lead to holy action. The message of repentance has been nearly forgotten in our day. To repent means to turn around. It involves a change of mind, attitude and conduct. It means to go back simply and humbly and start all over. David, the man after God's own heart, enjoyed thrilling companionship with God. During many careless periods of life he went his

125

own way: He saw a woman he wanted, he saw leadership he wanted, he saw power and status, and he connived to get what he wanted. The flesh asserted itself in all its ugliness. God said "No," but David said, "Yes," and he sinned greatly. The Scriptures ask, "Can two walk together, except they be agreed?" (Amos 3:3, KJV). The answer is emphatically, "*No!*" When David walked after his own desires, he walked without God. Many people think they walk with God when actually they have walked off and left Him, because they are living contrary to God's Word. In David's life, the glad day of repentance always dawned and David would cry, "Against thee, thee only, have I sinned and done this evil in thy sight" (Psalms 51:4, KJV). Each time David confessed his sin, immediately fellowship was restored, and God and David walked together once more. To confess means to say what God has said; to agree with God. David had said, "Lord, I'm wrong, and Thou art right." This is confession. This changed attitude results in a return in conduct to what John calls first works. This is repentance.

What does John mean by first works? Surely this means daily fellowship with God. First works also means to serve others in a spontaneous sharing of the things of God, to be mastered by the needs about us. First works are not stingy but generous. The redemptive *Word* which we take in our daily fellowship with God issues forth in a redemptive *work* to others. The world outside the church is weary of listening to us talk without feeling the concrete manifestations of our love. God's Holy Spirit can empower us to live and act as loudly as

126

we talk: first works is the twin of first love. Positive action in moving out of our own preoccupations to care for other people demonstrates our love for Jesus Christ. If this seems so very difficult, try praying specifically for someone you want to care about. Prayer often leads to love.

The Apostle John concludes with a severe warning, "I will come unto thee quickly, and will remove thy candlestick out of his place, except thou repent" (Revelation 2:5, KJV). Nevertheless, the Ephesians refused the message of John, and they suffered the consequences—removal!

I have personally witnessed Christians who have been removed by God because they refused to heed His rebuke, as were Ananias and Sapphira when they persisted in living a lie. To the Corinthians, who shared in the ordinance of the Lord's Table carelessly, Paul wrote, "For this cause many are weak and sickly among you, and many sleep" (I Corinthians 11:30, KJV). Obviously some of these were removed because they refused to change their careless ways.

Where is Ephesus today? Where is the light that once burned there intensely? The light is long gone, and the church of Ephesus exists no more. "Beloved," says Jude, "keep yourselves in the love of God" (v. 21, KJV). What more can we ask today?

> *Lord, help us to remember to repent our carelessness, our double living, our preoccupations with ourselves. Help us do first works in the flaming spirit of first love. We do want to move out in Thy love as*

we first did. We do want to be gripped by the needs of other people who are closed in on themselves. We want to introduce them to the warm force of Thy love which will cause their personalities to burst and blossom. Thank Thee for allowing us to commune together in prayer and in love. Make us fresh and new and alive again. All this we pray in the name of our wonderful Lord, Jesus Christ. Amen.

Rest awhile my busy servant
Sometimes in your busyness you forget Me!